A 40-Day Personal Journey
DAILY DEVOTIONAL AND JOURNAL

When Heaven INVADES Earth

A Practical Guide to a Life of Miracles

BILL JOHNSON

Text compiled by Jan Sherman.

Destiny Image® Publishers, Inc.

P.O. Box 310
Shippensburg, PA 17257-0310

*"Speaking to the Purposes of God for This Generation
and for the Generations to Come"*

ISBN 0-7684-2297-3

For Worldwide Distribution
Printed in the U.S.A.

This book and all other Destiny Image, Revival Press, MercyPlace, Fresh Bread, Destiny Image Fiction, and Treasure House books are available at Christian bookstores and distributors worldwide.

3 4 5 6 7 8 9 10 /11 10 09 08 07 06

To place a book order call
1-800-722-6774.

For more information on foreign distributors, call
717-532-3040.

Or reach us on the Internet:
www.destinyimage.com

Table of Contents

The Normal Christian Life

✤

FOR THE KINGDOM OF GOD IS NOT IN WORD BUT IN POWER (1 CORINTHIANS 4:20).

✤

Our church's deliberate pursuit of the poor and the miracles is common. [Working miracles] is closer to the normal Christian life than what the Church *normally* experiences. The lack of miracles isn't because it is not in God's will for us. The problem exists between our ears. As a result, a transformation—*a renewing of the mind*—is needed, and it's only possible through a work of the Holy Spirit that typically comes upon desperate people.

[Our church members] are ordinary people who serve an extravagant Father. [The only] great person involved [is] Jesus. All the rest of us simply make room for God, believing Him to be good 100 percent of the time. The risks that [we take are] more than God [can] pass up....

The company of people who have joined this quest for an authentic gospel—*the gospel of the Kingdom*—is increasing. Loving God and His people is an honor. We will no longer make up excuses for powerlessness because powerlessness is inexcusable. Our mandate is simple: raise up a generation that can openly display the raw power of God. [We are on a] quest for the King and His Kingdom.

(Quote From *When Heaven Invades Earth,* Pages 27-28)

QUESTIONS

1. What do you think helps create an *opportunity* for a miracle to happen?

2. In your opinion, why do contemporary local churches find signs and wonders to be less frequent than what the churches in the first century experienced?

3. How have miracles affected your life? Have you experienced a miracle or seen one? If so, was there an atmosphere for the supernatural? What was it like?

4. Who needs miracles in your sphere of influence? Be specific to name the person and the specific miracle needed. In your view, what is necessary to bring about each miracle?

5. Explain why salvation is the biggest miracle of all. Regarding the list you wrote for #4 above, are there any who need salvation? How might this miracle come to them?

6. The author tells us, "Loving God and His people is an honor." Have you ever thought of this as an honor? By adopting this attitude, how could Christians change the way they are viewed by those outside the Kingdom?

MEDITATION

*"The lack of miracles isn't because
it is not in God's will for us.
The problem exists between our ears"*
(*When Heaven Invades Earth*, Page 27).

*What miracles do you desire to see
God perform through you?
What do you think is your biggest
obstacle to seeing these manifest?
Pray for the Holy Spirit to bring
your mind into submission to
His wisdom and will.*

Commission Restored

THEN GOD BLESSED THEM, AND GOD SAID TO THEM, "BE FRUITFUL AND MULTIPLY; FILL THE EARTH AND SUBDUE IT; HAVE DOMINION OVER THE FISH OF THE SEA, OVER THE BIRDS OF THE AIR, AND OVER EVERY LIVING THING THAT MOVES ON THE EARTH" (GENESIS 1:28).

---

*T*he backbone of Kingdom authority and power is found in the *commission*. Discovering God's original commission and purpose for mankind can help to fortify our resolve to a life of history changing significance. To find that truth we must go back to the beginning.

Man was created in the image of God and placed into the Father's ultimate expression of beauty and peace: the Garden of Eden. Outside of that garden it was a different story. It was without the order and blessing contained within and was in great need of the touch of God's delegated one—Adam.

Adam and Eve were placed in the garden with a mission. God said, "Be fruitful and multiply; fill the earth and subdue it." It was God's intention that as they bore more children, who also lived under God's rule, they would be extending the boundaries of His garden (His government) through the simplicity of their devotion to Him. The greater the number of people in right relationship to God, the greater the impact of their leadership. This process was to continue until the entire earth was covered with the glorious rule of God through man.

(Quote From *When Heaven Invades Earth*, Page 30)

QUESTIONS

1. Why do you think God chose to delegate His authority on earth?

2. Do you think mankind (Adam and Eve) were fully prepared to handle their delegated authority? Why or why not?

3. The author tells us that simple devotion was all that was necessary for God's government to be extended. What are your thoughts as to how this can be true?

4. As God's delegated authority, what impact have you made to defeat darkness?

5. Do you feel as if you are one who subdues the earth, or are you subdued by it?

6. In what ways have you accepted your *commission* from the Lord? Are you resolved to a life of history changing significance? What does this mean to you?

MEDITATION

"In Genesis chapter 1 we discover it's not a perfect universe....It's obvious why the rest of the planet needed to be subdued—it was under the influence of darkness (see Gen. 1:2). God could have destroyed the devil and his host with a word, but instead He chose to defeat darkness through His delegated authority— those made in His image who were lovers of God by choice" (*When Heaven Invades Earth*, Page 30).

As someone who was created in the image of God, how can you use that image to subdue the earth?

We Are Born to Rule

And Jesus came and spoke to them, saying, "All authority has been given to Me in heaven and on earth. Go therefore and make disciples of all the nations, baptizing them in the name of the Father and of the Son and of the Holy Spirit" (Matthew 28:18-19).

*I*n redeeming man, Jesus retrieved what man had given away....The original plan was never aborted; it was fully realized once and for all in the resurrection and ascension of Jesus. We were then to be completely restored to His plan of ruling as a people made in His image. And as such we would learn how to enforce the victory obtained at Calvary....

We were born to rule—rule over creation, over darkness—to plunder hell and establish the rule of Jesus wherever we go by preaching the gospel of the Kingdom. *Kingdom* means: *King's domain.* In the original purpose of God, mankind ruled over creation. Now that sin has entered the world, creation has been infected by darkness, namely: disease, sickness, afflicting spirits, poverty, natural disasters, demonic influence, etc. Our rule is still over creation, but now it is focused on exposing and undoing the works of the devil. We are to give what we have received to reach that end. If I truly receive power from an encounter with the God of power, I am equipped to give it away. The invasion of God into impossible situations comes through a people who have received power from on high and learn to release it into the circumstances of life.

(Quote From *When Heaven Invades Earth,* Pages 32-33)

QUESTIONS

1. The author tells us that Jesus retrieved what man had given away. What was it that man gave away? At what cost?

2. How does a person increase his rule over darkness?

3. Have you ever "plundered hell"? What types of things might this include?

4. What does it take for us to expose and undo the works of the devil? What spiritual gifts might we use to do this?

5. Have you received power from an encounter with God? Is this power specialized in any specific arena? How can you expand it?

6. Do you readily release the power you have received into the circumstances of your life? What holds you back? What do you think is necessary to have a greater release?

MEDITATION

*"We are often more convinced of our **unworthiness** than we are of His **worth**. Our **inability** takes on greater focus than does His **ability**. But the same One who called **fearful Gideon** a Valiant Warrior and **unstable Peter** a Rock has called us the Body of His beloved Son on earth. That has to count for something"*

(*When Heaven Invades Earth*, Page 34).

Who do you relate to the most…Gideon or Peter? What ability do you find in Jesus that makes up for your inability?

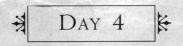

Repent to See

T HEREFORE, LEAVING THE DISCUSSION OF THE ELEMENTARY PRINCIPLES OF CHRIST, LET US GO ON TO PERFECTION, NOT LAYING AGAIN THE FOUNDATION OF REPENTANCE FROM DEAD WORKS AND OF FAITH TOWARD GOD (HEBREWS 6:1).

*J*esus the Messiah came…full of surprises. Only the contrite in heart could keep up with His constant *coloring outside the lines* and stay unoffended. His purpose was revealed in His primary message: "Repent, for the kingdom of heaven is at hand" (Mt. 4:17). Now there's something that caught them completely off guard; He brought His world with Him!

Repentance means much more than weeping over sin, or even turning from those sins to follow God. In fact, turning from sin to God is more the *result* of true repentance than it is the actual act. Repentance means you *change your way of thinking.* And it's only in changing the way we think that we can discover the focus of Jesus' ministry—the Kingdom.

This is not just a heavenly mandate to have happy thoughts. Obeying this command is possible only for those who surrender to the grace of God. The renewed mind is the result of a surrendered heart.

Repentance is often defined as *doing an about-face.* It implies that I was pursuing one direction in life and I change to pursue another. Scripture illustrates it like this, "Repentance from dead works…faith toward God" (Heb. 6:1). Faith then is both the crown and the enabler of repentance.

(Quote From *When Heaven Invades Earth,* Pages 37-38)

QUESTIONS

1. Why do you think Jesus "colored outside the lines"? Do you think you imitate Him in this way? Why or why not?

2. What does repentance mean to you? What takes place in your heart when you truly repent?

3. How easy is it to change your way of thinking about something of which you have always been sure? When you repent of something, how does it change your mind?

4. Why is the heart involved in order to renew the mind? How does this work?

5. How is obedience possible only for those who have a surrendered heart? How does someone surrender to God's grace?

6. How does faith enable repentance? Is God asking you to repent of some sin or disobedience? How does your faith need to grow in order to truly repent?

MEDITATION

*"Hidden sin is the **Achilles' heel** of the Church in this hour. It has kept us from the purity that breeds boldness and great faith"* (*When Heaven Invades Earth*, Page 38).

*Are there people in your life who you can count on to help you identify your hidden sins? Find one or two who can give you a current assessment of your **Achilles' heel**. Ask God to forgive you for these, even if you still do not see them yourself. Ask for boldness and great faith to have their work in your life.*

Dominion Realized

✠

BUT IF I CAST OUT DEMONS BY THE SPIRIT OF GOD, SURELY THE KINGDOM OF GOD HAS COME UPON YOU (MATTHEW 12:28).

✠

*T*he enemy's attempt to anchor our affections to the things that are visible is easily resisted when our hearts are aware of the presence of His world. Such awareness aids us in the task of being *co-laborers* (see 1 Cor. 3:9) with Christ—*destroying the works of the devil* (see 1 Jn. 3:8).

If the Kingdom is *here and now,* then we must acknowledge it's in the invisible realm....

The unseen world has influence over the visible. If the people of God will not reach for the Kingdom at hand, the realm of darkness is ready to display its ability to influence. The good news is that *"His* [the Lord's] *kingdom rules over all"* (Ps. 103:19).

Jesus illustrated this reality in Matthew 12:28, saying, "If I cast out demons by the Spirit of God, surely the kingdom of God has come upon you." There are two things to notice....First, Jesus worked only through the Spirit of God; and second, the kingdom of God came upon someone in his deliverance. Jesus caused the collision between two worlds: the world of darkness and the world of light. Darkness *always* gives way to light! And in the same way, when the dominion of God was released through Jesus to that man, he became free.

(Quote From *When Heaven Invades Earth,* Pages 38, 41)

QUESTIONS

1. How aware are you of the "presence of His world"? Why is this awareness a "heart" issue and not just a "mind" issue?

2. How does the awareness of God's world in our world help us to be *co-laborers* with Christ? Do you think of yourself as one who destroys the works of the devil? Why or why not?

3. How have you seen the invisible realm of the Kingdom of God? Have you seen it when others around you had not? What do you do when you see this realm?

4. In light of the fact that the world has so many difficult issues and there are multitudes who deny the existence of God, how do you explain Psalm 103:19: "*His kingdom rules over all*"?

5. Just as Jesus worked only through the Spirit of God, we need to do likewise as His agents. Evaluate your dependence upon the Spirit and how you operate as His agent in your daily life.

6. The collision between the world of darkness and the world of light will have repercussions for those who experience it. What was your world of darkness like and what happened when light invaded it? Who needs to hear your testimony this week? Today?

MEDITATION

*"**Grace** is different from the **Law***
*in that the favor comes **before** the obedience.*
Under grace the commandments of the Lord
come fully equipped with the ability to perform
them…to those who hear from the heart
(see Jas. 1:21-25). Grace enables what it commands"
(*When Heaven Invades Earth*, Page 41).

Do you feel the grace upon you when
you choose to obey in a way that is
normally difficult for you? Take time to praise
the God who enables you to obey all His commands.

Faith—Anchored In the Unseen

Now faith is the substance of things hoped for, the evidence of things not seen (Hebrews 11:1).

---

*F*aith has its anchor in the unseen realm. It lives *from* the invisible *toward* the visible. Faith actualizes what it realizes. The Scriptures contrast the life of faith with the limitations of natural sight (see 2 Cor. 5:7). Faith provides eyes for the heart.

Jesus expects people to see from the heart. He once called a group of religious leaders *hypocrites* because they could discern the weather but couldn't discern the times. It's obvious why Jesus would prefer people to recognize the *times* (spiritual climate and seasons) over natural weather conditions, but it's not quite so apparent why He would consider them hypocrites if they didn't.

Many of us have thought that the ability to see into the spiritual realm is more the result of a special gift than an unused potential of everyone. I remind you that Jesus addresses this charge to the Pharisees and Sadducees. The very fact that they, of all people, were required to see is evidence that everyone has been given this ability. They became blind to His dominion because of their own corrupted hearts and were judged for their unfulfilled potential....

Faith...is the nature of life in this family. Faith sees. It brings His Kingdom into focus. All of the Father's resources, all of His benefits, are accessible through faith.

(Quote From *When Heaven Invades Earth*, Pages 43-44)

QUESTIONS

1. Due to the fact that faith has its anchor in the unseen realm, how do you describe faith to an unbeliever?

2. What do you think the author means when he says, "Faith actualizes what it realizes"? What does this statement have to do with how you approach matters that you face in your daily life?

3. How does a person "see from the heart"? What spiritual gifts do we use when we recognize the times and seasons in our lives?

4. How would you rate your ability to see into the spiritual realm? What can you do to stimulate the unused potential you still possess?

5. What types of corruption do you face that can make you blind to Jesus' dominion? What steps might you take to avoid and/or divert from that corruption when it comes your way?

6. If "faith is the nature of life in this family," as a member of the family, what must you do to cultivate the culture of faith? What kind of commitment do you need to make?

MEDITATION

*"Jesus told us that He only did what He **saw***
His Father do. Such an insight is vital for those
who want more. The power of His actions, for instance, the
mud in the eye of the blind, is rooted in His ability to see"
(*When Heaven Invades Earth*, Page 44).

Look up several Scriptures that speak of the focus
of our spiritual eyes—Matthew 6:33;
Colossians 3:2; 2 Corinthians 4:18.
Pray that the principles of these verses would be
like corrective laser surgery to your spiritual eyes.

Faith From a Relationship

B Y FAITH WE UNDERSTAND THAT THE WORLDS WERE FRAMED BY THE WORD OF GOD, SO THAT THE THINGS WHICH ARE SEEN WERE NOT MADE OF THINGS WHICH ARE VISIBLE (HEBREWS 11:3).

---

*F*aith is born of the Spirit in the hearts of mankind. Faith is neither intellectual nor anti-intellectual. It is superior to the intellect. The Bible does not say, *with the mind man believes!* Through faith, man is able to come into agreement with the mind of God....

The Holy Spirit lives in my spirit. That is the place of communion with God. As we learn to receive from our spirits we learn how to be Spirit led.

"By faith, we understand" (Heb. 11:3). Faith is the foundation for all true intellectualism. When we *learn to learn* that way, we open ourselves up to grow in true faith because faith does not require understanding to function.

I'm sure that most of you have had this experience—you've been reading the Bible, and a verse *jumps out at you.* There is great excitement over this verse that seems to give so much life and encouragement to you. Yet initially you couldn't teach or explain that verse if your life depended on it. What happened is this: Your spirit received the life-giving power of the word from the Holy Spirit (see 2 Cor. 3:6). When we learn to receive from our spirit, our mind becomes the student and is therefore subject to the Holy Spirit. Through the process of revelation and experience our mind eventually obtains understanding. That is biblical learning—the spirit giving influence to the mind.

(Quote From *When Heaven Invades Earth,* Pages 46-47)

QUESTIONS

1. Describe how you view faith in regard to your mind and intellect. How do you see the tug-of-war that plays between the intellect and your faith? How can it be a win/win outcome?

2. We know that God's wisdom is beyond man's wisdom; so why do we rely on our minds so much? What can help us come into agreement with the mind of God?

3. Take stock of your current place of communion with God. Does it flow easily, or do you find life scarce? Does the Spirit of God find a welcome domain with your spirit? Do you move together as one?

4. The author tells us, "Faith is the foundation for all true intellectualism." Explain this in terms of how you understand the truth of the Kingdom of God.

5. When you read the Bible, does the Holy Spirit provide life-giving power to the words you read? How does this work? What lets you know that it is the Holy Spirit speaking?

6. To become a student of the Holy Spirit, how is humility involved? What is your understanding of the process of revelation and experience, and their impact on your understanding?

MEDITATION

*"Faith is the mirror of the heart that reflects
the realities of His world into ours. It is the substance
of the unseen realm. This wonderful gift from God is the
initial earthly manifestation of what exists in His
Kingdom. It is a testimony of an invisible realm called
the Kingdom of God. Through prayer we are able to pull
that reality into this one—that is how faith functions"*
(*When Heaven Invades Earth*, Page 48).

*Take some time to reflect on the realities of God's world
and how they have invaded your world. Pray specifically
for areas that need the reality of the Kingdom of God today.*

A Superior Reality

✣

SET YOUR MIND ON THINGS ABOVE, NOT ON THINGS ON THE EARTH (COLOSSIANS 3:2).

✣

*M*y faith is not just an abiding faith; it is active. It is aggressive by nature. It has focus and purpose. Faith grabs hold of the reality of the Kingdom and forcefully and violently brings it into a collision with this natural one. An inferior kingdom cannot stand.

One of the more common things people tell me when I'm about to pray for their healing is, *I know God can do it.* So does the devil. At best that is hope...not faith. Faith knows He will.

For one who has faith, there is nothing impossible. There are no impossibilities when there is faith...and there are no exceptions....

"So then faith comes by hearing, and hearing by the word of God" (Rom. 10:17). Notice it does not say, *faith comes from having heard.* The whole nature of faith implies a relationship with God that is current. The emphasis is on hearing...in the now!...

What this world needs is for the Church to return to a *show and tell* message on the kingdom of God. They need an anchor that is greater than everything they can see. The world system has no answers to the world's increasing problems—every solution is only temporary.

(Quote From *When Heaven Invades Earth,* Pages 51-53)

QUESTIONS

1. Define "abiding faith" and "active faith." How does an active faith become aggressive? Does this describe your faith?

2. Does "forceful" and "violent" describe your faith? Do you have collisions with the natural world? How is the natural world inferior to God's Kingdom?

3. Explain the difference between hope and faith. Which characterizes your worldview for the most part? How can you increase your faith level on a daily basis?

4. If "there are no impossibilities when there is faith," why do you think there are so few miracles? Why does the Church seem so impotent?

5. The progression of faith as stated in Romans 10:17 elevates the importance of the Word of God, "So then faith comes by hearing, and hearing by the word of God." Is there a difference between reading and hearing? How do you think this relates to Hebrews 4:12, "For the word of God is living and powerful..."?

6. Is the Kingdom of God something that most Christians choose to "show and tell"? How can Christians change their mind-set to understand the permanence of the Kingdom solutions to today's problems and the temporary nature of the world system?

MEDITATION

"People of great faith are hard to live with.
*Their reasoning is **otherworldly***"
(*When Heaven Invades Earth*, Page 51).

In what ways have you found people of great
faith difficult to live with? Does your description
*resemble yourself in any way? Does **otherworldly***
mean to be so heavenly minded that we are no earthly
good? How can we be "in the world but not of it"?

The Cluster Bomb Effect

N OR GIVE PLACE TO THE DEVIL (EPH-
ESIANS 4:27).

*F*aith is not the absence of doubt; it's the presence of belief. I may not always feel that I have great faith. It's a mistake for me to ever examine my faith. I seldom find it. It's better for me to obey *quickly*. After it's over I can look back and see that my obedience came from faith.

When the corporate level of faith grows, it has what I call a *cluster bomb effect,* where innocent bystanders get touched by the miracle-working power of God....

Corporate faith pulls on heaven in marvelous ways. His world becomes manifest all around us....

But power is not in the number of people in attendance. It's the number of people in agreement. Exponential power (see Deut. 32:30) is the product of the *unity of faith*....

An automobile may have several hundred horsepower. But the car will go nowhere until the clutch is released, connecting the power contained in the running motor and transferring that power to the wheels. So it is with faith. We have all the power of heaven behind us. But it is our faith that connects what is available to the circumstances at hand. Faith takes what is available and makes it actual.

(Quote From *When Heaven Invades Earth,* Pages 53-55)

QUESTIONS

1. If "faith is not the absence of doubt," how do we get rid of doubts? Do you find that thoughts of doubt come into your mind when you pray for miracles?

2. If faith is "the presence of belief," how do we make faith operational in our daily lives? What fights against you to keep you from surrounding yourself with faith wherever you go?

3. What has your experience been in terms of the corporate working of faith? Have you ever experienced "innocent bystander" touches of God's power? What brings these types of corporate anointing?

4. What comes to mind when you think about the Kingdom of God becoming manifest on the earth? Is your picture filled with a serene sedentary group of people enjoying the "best" earth has to offer, or is it painted with hard work, violence, and corporate revolution? Which picture do you choose to be part of?

5. Why do you think power increases exponentially when people unify their faith? What scriptural principle is at work?

6. As you trace your history, how do you see your faith connecting to the power of heaven? What are your hopes for the future of your connection?

MEDITATION

The author tells us, "Rest is the climate that faith
grows in"(see Heb. 3:11–4:11). But he also says,
"Faith may quietly press in, or it may cry out very loudly,
but it is always violent in the spirit world (see Mt. 11:12)"
(*When Heaven Invades Earth*, Pages 54-55).

Where are you in the tension between rest and
violence? How does Jesus want to bring balance
to your life and encourage you forward?

Praying Heaven Down

Iᴺ ᴛʜɪꜱ ᴍᴀɴɴᴇʀ, ᴛʜᴇʀᴇꜰᴏʀᴇ, ᴘʀᴀʏ: Oᴜʀ Fᴀᴛʜᴇʀ ɪɴ ʜᴇᴀᴠᴇɴ, Hᴀʟʟᴏᴡᴇᴅ ʙᴇ Yᴏᴜʀ ɴᴀᴍᴇ (Mᴀᴛᴛʜᴇᴡ 6:9).

---

*T*he Lord's Model Prayer provides the clearest instruction on how we bring the reality of His world into this one. The generals of revival speak to us from ages past saying, *If you pray, He will come!*

Biblical prayer is always accompanied by radical obedience. God's response to prayer with obedience always releases the nature of heaven into our impaired circumstances.

Jesus' model reveals the only two real priorities of prayer: First, intimacy with God that is expressed in worship—*holy is Your name.* And second, to bring His Kingdom to earth, establishing His dominion over the needs of mankind—*Your Kingdom come.…*

Let me highlight one more thought that will help us to better understand the purpose behind prayer; as disciples we are both citizens and ambassadors of another world. This world is our assignment, but not our home. Our purpose is eternal. The resources needed to complete the assignment are unlimited. The only restrictions are those between our ears. …

An outline of Matthew 6:9-13 gives us the Kingdom approach to prayer:

I.   Praise and worship

II. Praying for heaven on earth

    A. Heaven's effect on material needs

    B. Heaven's effect on personal relationships

    C. Heaven's effect on our relationship to evil

III. Praise and worship

(Quote From *When Heaven Invades Earth,* Pages 58, 62)

QUESTIONS

1. How does the Lord's Prayer help us "bring the reality of His world into this one"? Has this been so in your experience?

2. Do you feel that the Lord comes when you pray? What is necessary for you to sense His presence during your prayer time?

3. The author gives us a progression—biblical prayer; radical obedience; release of heaven into our impaired circumstances. Comment on this progression in terms of your personal experience.

4. The first priority of prayer is to minister to God out of an intimate personal relationship. How much of your prayer time is spent in worship? What are the ways in which you hallow His name?

5. The second priority of prayer is to bring the reality of His rulership (the Kingdom) to earth. How do you pray His Kingdom come? Where do you need His Kingdom to reign in your life currently?

6. As ambassadors of another world, we are to remember our purpose is eternal. Having an eternal perspective can change how we view our daily interaction with others and our mundane chores. In what ways can you put this eternal perspective to use in your life?

❧ MEDITATION ❧

*"If you want anything from God, you will have
to pray into heaven. That is where it all is. If you
live in the earth realm and expect to receive from God,
you will never get anything"* (Albert Hibbert on
Smith Wigglesworth, *The Secret of His Power,*
Tulsa, OK: Harrison House, Inc., 1982, page 47)
(*When Heaven Invades Earth*, Page 57).

*Consider this quote from Smith Wigglesworth
in terms of how you currently pray.
If you are not to live in the earth realm,
where are you to live? How do you arrive there?*

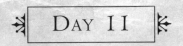

DAY 11

Representing Another World

FOR OUR CITIZENSHIP IS IN HEAVEN, FROM WHICH WE ALSO EAGERLY WAIT FOR THE SAVIOR, THE LORD JESUS CHRIST (PHILIPPIANS 3:20).

When we pray for His Kingdom to come, we are asking Him to superimpose the rules, order, and benefits of His world over this one until this one looks like His....[God's] world collides with the world of darkness, and His world always wins. Our battle is always a battle for dominion—a conflict of kingdoms....

God has chosen to work through us. We are His delegated authority on planet earth, and prayer is the vehicle that gives occasion for His invasion. Those who don't pray allow darkness to continue ruling. The enemy's greatest efforts at deceiving the Church are centered on the purpose and effect of prayer.

"For our citizenship is in heaven, from which we also eagerly wait for the Savior, the Lord Jesus Christ" (Phil. 3:20). Paul spoke these words to the church at Philippi, a Roman city in the country of Macedonia. It enjoyed a Roman culture and the rule and protection of Roman government, all while living in Macedonia. Philippians understood very well Paul's charge about being citizens of another world. Paul spoke, not about going to heaven someday, but about living as citizens of heaven today...specifically *from heaven toward earth.*

We have the privilege of representing heaven *in* this world, so that we might bring a manifestation of heaven *to* this world.

(Quote From *When Heaven Invades Earth,* Pages 63-64)

QUESTIONS

1. Our society wants to whitewash the collision God's world has with ours by compromising Kingdom values with humanism. How do you recognize when compromise threatens your convictions? What should we do about it?

2. If God's world always wins in the fight over darkness, why do we see so much darkness in the world today? What is stopping us from seeing a greater degree of victory? What is our responsibility in this?

3. What role does prayer play in the war of the worlds (God's versus darkness)? What has your prayer life done toward this cause? How can you influence others to join their prayers with yours in order to bring victory to this world?

4. As a citizen of heaven, what are we waiting for? (see Phil. 3:20) What does living as "citizens of heaven today" on earth look like? What affect can it have?

5. God has asked us to do the following jobs. Describe how you are currently fulfilling each one and where you need to grow the most.
   - ambassador
   - invasion force
   - infiltrator
   - citizen
   - warrior

MEDITATION

*"When we pray for His Kingdom to come,
we are asking Him to superimpose the rules,
order, and benefits of His world over this
one until this one looks like His"*
(*When Heaven Invades Earth*, Page 63).

*If you were to pick one area where you feel
God's Kingdom needs to be superimposed as soon
as possible, what would it be? Are there other people
you know who have this same burden? Could you join
with them in corporate prayer to allow exponential power
to make its impact? Plan to contact them and pray in unity.*

DAY 12

Embassy Lifestyle

❖

E VERY PLACE THAT THE SOLE OF YOUR FOOT
WILL TREAD UPON I HAVE GIVEN YOU...
(JOSHUA 1:3).

❖

*A*s ambassadors we live in one world while representing another. An embassy is the headquarters of an ambassador and his or her staff. It is actually considered a part of the nation it represents. So it is with the believer/ambassador. The Bible promises: *"Every place that the sole of your foot will tread upon I have given you"* (Josh. 1:3).

Just as ambassadors of the United States have an income based on the standard of living of this nation regardless of what nation they serve in, so also ambassadors of the Kingdom of God live according to the economy of heaven, though they are still on earth. All of our King's resources are at our disposal to carry out His will. That is how Jesus could speak of the carefree life—*consider the sparrow* (see Mt. 6:26).

As an ambassador, the military of the Kingdom I represent is at my disposal to help me carry out the King's orders. If as a representative of a nation my life is threatened, all of my government's military might is prepared to do whatever necessary to protect and deliver me. So it is with the heaven's angelic host. They *render service for those who would inherit salvation* (see Heb. 1:14).

(Quote From *When Heaven Invades Earth,* Page 65)

QUESTIONS

1. What are the types of considerations United States ambassadors must give as they represent our country, yet respect and live in another culture? What types of considerations must we entertain as ambassadors of the Kingdom of God while living in this world?

2. Make a list of the places where your feet tread in a typical day. How can you make your "embassy" real in these places? What kind of awareness will you need?

3. If all of our King's resources are at our disposal, how should we be stewards of His resources? What should our mind-set be so that we won't be unbalanced—thinking ourselves in poverty, or spending as if there was no tomorrow?

4. Who are the "military of the Kingdom"? How does the Lord's armed forces work on our behalf? What types of protection might they give? What kinds of deliverance might they provide? Have you called on the angelic host to help you at times? What kinds of service did they render?

5. As you consider your life as an ambassador, remember the protocol that is given to respect and honor diplomats. Do you think there is a respect for Kingdom diplomats in the spiritual world? In the earthly realm? Why or why not?

6. How carefree are you? (See Matthew 6:26.) What concerns do you have that make it difficult to experience the resources of the King?

MEDITATION

*The author shares, "This **ambassador mentality**
is one I first picked up from Winkey Pratney.
When he boards a plane, he reminds himself
that while others may represent IBM and XEROX,
he is there representing another world. I have followed
his example and practiced this principle for close
to thirty years. It has helped me to keep a clear
perspective on the eternal purpose of every outing"*
(*When Heaven Invades Earth*, Page 65).

*How might you prepare your mind
every day to have an **ambassador mentality**?*

The Kingdom and the Spirit

❖

T O KNOW THE LOVE OF CHRIST WHICH PASSES KNOWLEDGE; THAT YOU MAY BE FILLED WITH ALL THE FULLNESS OF GOD (EPHESIANS 3:19).

❖

*J*ohn the Baptist was the *high water mark* for all under the Old Covenant. But the least in this new era were born to surpass Him through their relationship with the Holy Spirit....

Likewise, salvation was not the ultimate goal of Christ's coming. It was the immediate target...the marker in the lane. Without accomplishing redemption, there was no hope for the ultimate goal—which was to fill each born again person with the Holy Spirit. God's desire is for the believer to overflow with Himself, that we might "...*be filled with all the fullness of God*" (Eph. 3:19). The resulting fullness of the Spirit was different than anyone had ever before experienced. For that reason, the greatest of all Old Testament prophets could confess: "I need to be baptized by you," meaning, "I need your baptism...the one I was assigned to announce!"

The baptism in the Holy Spirit makes a lifestyle available to us that not even John had access to. Consider this: we could travel off of this planet in any direction at the speed of light, 186,000 miles a second, for billions of years, and never begin to exhaust what we already know to exist. All of that rests in the palm of His hand. And it's this God who wants to fill us with His fullness. That ought to make a difference!

(Quote From *When Heaven Invades Earth*, Pages 69, 71)

QUESTIONS

1. Explain the difference between the Old Covenant and the New Covenant. What made John the "high water mark" for the Old Covenant? Why was this mark less than what God intended for us?

2. How does a person develop a relationship with the Holy Spirit? Describe your current relationship with the Spirit of God. How has He shaped your world internally and externally?

3. How does salvation in Jesus Christ open the door for the Holy Spirit to fill a person? What has been your experience with receiving salvation and the infilling of the Holy Spirit?

4. When Ephesians 3:19 tells us to "be filled with all the fullness of God," what does this mean? How can any imperfect person on earth be filled with God? What does this mean for your life?

5. How does it make you feel to consider that the same God, who holds the universe in the palm of His hand, wants to have intimate communion with you?

6. Knowing that the Almighty God desires to fill us should keep our egos in a true balance...humble but bold, full of faith and yet full of submission. Instead of evaluating your "self-worth," evaluate your "God-worth."

❧ MEDITATION ❧

*"Somehow I always thought that the baptism
in the Holy Spirit was a one-time event; I received
my prayer language and that was it. The Bible
teaches differently. In Acts 2, we find 120 being baptized
in the Spirit in the upper room. Yet, in Acts 4 we find
some of the same crowd being **refilled**. Some have put
it this way: one baptism, many fillings. Why? We leak"*
(*When Heaven Invades Earth*, Page 72).

*Take some moments to reflect
on where your leaks are. How can they be patched?*

The Value of His Presence

A ND LO, I AM WITH YOU ALWAYS, EVEN TO THE END OF THE AGE (MATTHEW 28:20B).

By far the greatest gift ever received by us is the Holy Spirit Himself. Those who discover the value of His presence enter realms of intimacy with God never previously considered possible. Out of this vital relationship arises a ministry of power that formerly was only a dream. The incomprehensible becomes possible because He is with us.

I will be with you is a promise made by God to all His servants. Moses heard it when he faced the challenge of delivering Israel from Egypt (see Ex. 3:12). Joshua received this promise when he led Israel into the Promised Land (see Josh. 1:9). When Gideon received the call of God to be a deliverer for Israel, God sealed it with the same promise (see Judg. 6:16). In the New Testament, this promise came to all believers through the Great Commission (see Mt. 28:19). It comes when God has required something of us that is humanly impossible. It's important to see this. It's the Presence of God that links us to the impossible. I tell our folks, *He is in me for my sake, but He's upon me for yours.* His presence makes anything possible!

God doesn't have to try to do supernatural things. He is supernatural. He would have to try to not be. If He is invited to a situation, we should expect nothing but supernatural invasion.

(Quote From *When Heaven Invades Earth,* Page 74)

QUESTIONS

1. How has the Holy Spirit increased your intimacy with God? In what ways has this changed your devotional time?

2. Has a new level of power accompanied your increase of intimacy? Power to do what?

3. When the Lord Jesus said He would always be with us, what did He mean? Have you felt Jesus with you in most of your walk? Why or why not?

4. Have you faced a challenge and needed deliverance? How did God bring deliverance? Was Jesus' presence a factor in your deliverance?

5. Have you had to lead others into a new area (on the job or in ministry or in the home) and needed courage to proceed? How did God build your leadership? Was Jesus' presence a factor in your ability to lead?

6. How has God worked the supernatural on your behalf or on behalf of someone you know? How do you explain to others how God supercedes the impossible and makes things possible?

❧ MEDITATION ❧

*"Following the leading of the Holy Spirit
can present us with [a] dilemma. While He
never contradicts His Word, He is very comfortable
contradicting our understanding of it....But to
follow Him, we must be willing to follow
off the map—to go beyond what we know. To do so
successfully we must recognize His presence above all."
How easily do you follow the Holy Spirit "off the map"?*
(*When Heaven Invades Earth*, Page 76).

Do you recognize His presence quickly?

The Anointing and the Antichrist Spirit

JESUS SAID TO THEM, "MY FOOD IS TO DO THE will of HIM WHO SENT ME, AND TO FINISH HIS WORK" (JOHN 4:34).

---

*I*t would seem that with all the significance attached to the name "Jesus," anyone desiring to undermine His work of redemption might be referred to as "Anti-Jesus," not "Anti-Christ." Even religious cults recognize the value of Jesus the man. At the very least, cults consider Him to be a teacher or a prophet and possibly "a" son of God. This horrendous error provides us with an understanding of why *antichrist* was the name given to this spirit of opposition. The spirits of hell are at war against the anointing, for without the anointing mankind is no threat to their dominion.

Jesus' concern for mankind was applauded. His humility was revered, but it was the anointing that released the supernatural. And it was the supernatural invasion of God Himself that was rejected by the religious leaders. This anointing is actually the person of the Holy Spirit upon someone to equip them for supernatural endeavors. So revered is the Holy Spirit in the Godhead, that Jesus said, "Anyone who speaks a word against the Son of Man, it will be forgiven him; but whoever speaks against the Holy Spirit, it will not be forgiven him, either in this age or in the age to come" (Mt. 12:32).

(Quote From *When Heaven Invades Earth*, Page 80)

QUESTIONS

1. Do you readily perceive when an antichrist spirit is at work? In what ways have you observed this? Why do so many people buy into the philosophy of antichrist?

2. Why do cults and others recognize Jesus as a teacher or a prophet? Why can't this be true? How does the spirit of antichrist take Jesus' anointing out of the picture?

3. How does our anointing threaten the dominion of the spirits of hell? Do you think of yourself as a threat? How much of a threat are you? Where do you need to become more of a threat?

4. Why do you think the supernatural acts of Jesus were rejected by the religious leaders in His day? Do you think the supernatural is rejected today? Why or why not?

5. How does the Holy Spirit equip someone for supernatural endeavors? How have you been equipped? Do you utilize that equipping regularly?

6. Why do you think the Holy Spirit is to be so revered? Explain Matthew 12:32 as you would to someone who doesn't understand the working of the Holy Spirit.

❧ MEDITATION ❧

*"To fulfill His mission, Jesus needed
the Holy Spirit....If the Son of God was that
reliant upon the anointing, His behavior should
clarify our need for the Holy Spirit's presence upon
us to do what the Father has assigned....We must
be clothed with the Holy Spirit for supernatural ministry"*
(*When Heaven Invades Earth*, Page 80).

*Just like the Old Testament priests, our anointing
qualifies us for ministry. Do you think most
Christians qualify their ministry with education
and/or position, or do they really see the anointing
as their qualification? What place does training
and equipping have in seeing God's purposes
fulfilled through us? How do you view your
ministry currently? Are you anointed?*

The Realm Beyond Reason

"FOR MY THOUGHTS ARE NOT YOUR THOUGHTS, NOR ARE YOUR WAYS MY WAYS," SAYS THE LORD. "FOR AS THE HEAVENS ARE HIGHER THAN THE EARTH, SO ARE MY WAYS HIGHER THAN YOUR WAYS, AND MY THOUGHTS THAN YOUR THOUGHTS" (ISAIAH 55:8-9).

*F*ollowing the anointing…is very similar to Israel following the cloud of the Lord's presence in the wilderness. The Israelites had no control over Him. He led, and the people followed. Wherever He went, supernatural activities took place. If they departed from the cloud, the miracles that sustained them would be gone. Can you imagine what would have happened if our fear-oriented theologians had been there? They would have created new doctrines explaining why the supernatural ministry that brought them out of Egypt was no longer necessary to bring them into the Promised Land. After all, now they had the tablets of stone. Then, as today, the real issue is the priority we place upon His presence. When that's intact, the supernatural abounds, but without it we have to make up new doctrines for why we're OK as we are.

In New Testament terms, being a people focused on His presence means that we are willing to live beyond reason. Not impulsively or foolishly, for these are poor imitations for real faith. The realm beyond reason is the world of obedience to God. Obedience is the expression of faith, and faith is our claim ticket to the God realm.…His nature is powerful and righteous, but His ways cannot be controlled. He is unpredictable.

(Quote From *When Heaven Invades Earth*, Page 82)

QUESTIONS

1. If you had been an Israelite in the wilderness, how would you have felt being at the Lord's mercy for everything you needed? Do you think their lack of control is why they continually questioned what the Lord was doing?

2. Have you ever wanted the Lord to tell you what, where, when, and how to do something? The Israelites had these answers, but they rebelled at the Lord's directives anyway. Do you think you would rebel if the Lord told you something that you didn't agree with? Why or why not?

3. What are some of the arguments you have heard that discount the supernatural activities of God, whether past or present? Why do you believe in God's supernatural power? What is your testimony to His power?

4. The cloud of God's presence marked the spot of His supernatural care for His people, the Israelites. How does the cloud of God's presence mark the spot of His supernatural care for His people today? Have you witnessed this presence and accompanying miracles? Describe your experience.

5. Does your rational mind ever keep you from realizing His presence at times? How does a world beyond reason work? How can you be sure it is real?

6. Explain the connection between obedience and faith. Do you find obedience difficult in any areas of your life? Is your faith affected in these same areas? What can you do to increase obedience and your faith?

❧ MEDITATION ❦

*"Every time we follow the leading of the
Holy Spirit, we fly in the face of the antichrist
spirit. While the foolishness of some who claim
to be Spirit-led have made this adventure
more difficult, we nevertheless are assured of
succeeding if it is truly our passionate desire.
He'll not give a stone to anyone who asks for bread"*
(*When Heaven Invades Earth*, Page 85).

*Take time to pray that the Lord will help you
follow and obey the leading of the Holy Spirit.
Ask Him to increase your passion to be Spirit-led.*

Teaching Into an Encounter

D O YOU NOT BELIEVE THAT I AM IN THE
FATHER, AND THE FATHER IN ME? THE
WORDS THAT I SPEAK TO YOU I DO NOT SPEAK
ON MY OWN AUTHORITY; BUT THE FATHER WHO
DWELLS IN ME DOES THE WORKS (JOHN 14:10).

*J*esus established the ultimate example in ministry by combining the proclamation of the gospel with signs and wonders. Matthew records this phenomenon this way: "And Jesus went about all Galilee, teaching in their synagogues, preaching the gospel of the kingdom, and healing all kinds of sickness and all kinds of disease among the people" (Mt. 4:23)....

The Gospel of John records how this combination of words and supernatural works takes place, "The words that I speak to you I do not speak on My own authority; but the Father who dwells in Me does the works" (Jn. 14:10). It's apparent that we speak the word, and the Father *does the works*—miracles!

As men and women of God who teach, we must require from ourselves *doing, with power*! And this *doing* must include a breaking into the impossible—through signs and wonders.

Bible teachers are to instruct in order to explain *what they just did,* or *are about to do.* Those who restrict themselves to mere words limit their gift, and may unintentionally lead believers to pride by increasing knowledge without an increased awareness of God's presence and power. It's in the trenches of Christ-like ministry that we learn to become totally dependent upon God. Moving in the impossible through relying on God short-circuits the development of pride.

(Quote From *When Heaven Invades Earth,* Pages 87-88)

QUESTIONS

1. If Jesus gave us the "ultimate example in ministry by combining the proclamation of the gospel with signs and wonders," why do you think we aren't able to continue in His footsteps? How does the partnership of the Word and wonders work?

2. When you speak the Word of God, on whose authority do you speak? How do you know that authority exists? What effect does the Word of God have?

3. When you do the works of God, on whose authority do you act? How do you know that authority exists? What effect does a true work of God have?

4. If we are to require ourselves to go about "*doing, with power,*" what must happen in the faith realm? What will equip us to extend our borders in the miraculous?

5. How can Bible teachers unintentionally lead believers into pride? Have you experienced this firsthand? What is the danger of knowledge without the awareness of God's presence and power?

6. Dependence upon God is the key to our encounters with the Almighty. How does relying on God short-circuit the development of pride?

MEDITATION

"Any revelation from God's Word
that does not lead us to an encounter with
God only serves to make us more religious.
The Church cannot afford 'form without power,'
for it creates Christians without purpose"
(*When Heaven Invades Earth*, Page 87).

How true is this for you? For your
local church? How can this change?

God Is Bigger Than His Book

❖

YOU ARE WRONG BECAUSE YOU KNOW NEITHER THE SCRIPTURES NOR GOD'S POWER (MATTHEW 22:29 NLT).

❖

*I*n this passage Jesus rebukes the Pharisees for their ignorance of the Scriptures *and* God's power. His rebuke comes within the context of *marriage* and *resurrection,* but is aimed at the ignorance infecting every area of their lives.

What was the cause? They didn't allow the Scriptures to lead them to God. They didn't understand…not really understand. The word *know* in this passage speaks of "personal experience." They tried to learn apart from such an experience. They were the champions of those who spent time studying God's Word. But their study didn't lead them to an encounter with God. It became an end in itself.

The Holy Spirit is the *dunamis* of heaven. An encounter with God is often a power encounter. Such encounters vary from person to person according to God's design. And it's the lack of power encounters that lead to a misunderstanding of God and His Word. Experience is necessary in building a true knowledge of the Word. Many fear experience because it *might* lead away from Scripture. The mistakes of some have led many to fear experiential pursuit. But it is illegitimate to allow fear to keep us from pursuing a deeper experience with God! Embracing such fear causes a failure to the other extreme, which is culturally more acceptable, but significantly worse in eternity.

(Quote From *When Heaven Invades Earth,* Page 92)

QUESTIONS

1. Do you think there are modern-day "Pharisees" within the Church who do not allow the Scriptures to lead them to God? What makes the ultimate difference to gain true understanding? How does this lead you to pray for the Church?

2. How does someone have a "personal experience" with God? How does a personal experience lead to understanding? Do you wonder at great preachers who find seemingly "new" truths hidden within Scriptures you have read many times? Is this because they allow the Scriptures to lead them into a personal experience and as a result they receive insight? How does this happen?

3. What place does study of God's Word have in the life of the believer? What is its limitation? What place does it have in your life?

4. Describe what a "power encounter" with God is like. Have you had one (or more) of these encounters? What makes them bring truth to light?

5. Why do people fear experiences? Are they justified by what they have experienced or seen others do? How can we avoid this pitfall?

6. What should replace any fear we have of power encounters with God? What are the risk factors if we *don't* have these encounters? What are the risks if we *do* have them?

❧ MEDITATION ❦

"The Bible is the absolute Word of God.
It reveals God; the obvious, the unexplainable,
the mysterious, and sometimes offensive.
It all reveals the greatness of our God. Yet it does
not contain Him. God is bigger than His book"
(*When Heaven Invades Earth*, Page 92).

Take time to praise God for His Word.
Give Him glory for its directives for your life. Then
worship the Lord for who He is in all of His greatness.

The Works of the Father

✠

A ND HE WHO SENT ME IS WITH ME. THE
FATHER HAS NOT LEFT ME ALONE, FOR I
ALWAYS DO THOSE THINGS THAT PLEASE HIM
(JOHN 8:29).

✠

*F*or hundreds of years the prophets spoke of the Messiah's coming. They gave over 300 specific details describing Him. Jesus fulfilled them all! The angels also gave witness to His divinity when they came with a message for the shepherds: "For there is born to you this day...a Savior, who is Christ the Lord" (Lk. 2:11). Nature itself testified to the arrival of the Messiah with the star that led the wise men (see Mt. 2:1). Yet with this one statement, "Unless I do the works of the Father, do not believe Me," (Jn. 10:37) Jesus put the credibility of all these *messengers* on the line. Their ministries would have been in vain without one more ingredient to confirm who He really was. That ingredient was *miracles*.

Jesus gave people the right to disbelieve it all if there was no demonstration of power upon His ministry. I hunger for the day when the Church will make the same statement to the world. *If we're not doing the miracles that Jesus did, you don't have to believe us....*

Jesus displayed the Father's heart. All His actions were earthly expressions of His Father in heaven....Jesus continues to point the way to the Father. It has now become our job, by means of the Holy Spirit, to discover and display the Father's heart: giving life, and destroying the works of the devil.

(Quote From *When Heaven Invades Earth,* Pages 97, 100)

QUESTIONS

1. The criteria Jesus gave in order to believe Him was fairly simple...He had to do the works of the Father. What are the works of the Father? How can someone recognize them when they see them?

2. Why does a demonstration of power bring credibility to ministry? Does this mean that anyone who does miracles is doing the work of the Father? Why or why not?

3. Why do miracles express the Father's heart? If the Church is to express the Father's heart to the world, it seems logical then, that they are to perform miracles. In your opinion, what is stopping the Church from doing this?

4. What types of miracles destroy the works of the devil? Explain. When a miracle happens, how does life and light go forth into darkness?

5. How adept are you at displaying the love of God through miracles? Where might you grow to increase your effectiveness in this arena? Create a plan to challenge yourself to greater dependence upon the Father for these kinds of works.

6. The author emphasizes how important doing the works of the Father is, by comparing all the credentials Jesus had (prophetic voices, angelic witnesses, and nature's testimonials), to this one overarching credential. In your opinion, why did God bother to do all these other proofs of Jesus' divinity? Do you see their purpose within the context of His greatest credential?

MEDITATION

"We can travel the globe and preach the gospel, but without a personal revelation of the Father's heart we're carrying around secondhand news—a story without a relationship. It might save people because it is truth, but there is so much more"
(*When Heaven Invades Earth*, Page 101).

What is your personal revelation?
Can you relate it easily if asked?

Everyone Is a Candidate

SO JESUS SAID TO THEM AGAIN, "PEACE TO YOU! AS THE FATHER HAS SENT ME, I ALSO SEND YOU" (JOHN 20:21).

---

*I*n the same way that Jesus revealed the Father's heart to Israel, so the Church is to *be a manifestation* of the Father's heart to the world....

Everyone in our community is a target for God's love. There are no exceptions. The testimonies of radical transformation come from every sector of society and every conceivable place—school, work, home, the malls and stores, and even the parks, streets, and homeless camps. Why? There is a growing company of people who have the Father's business in mind. They consciously take Him wherever they go....Every believer has a part to play in carrying out this privileged assignment.

We have the privilege of rediscovering God's original purpose for His people. We who long for this must pursue Him with reckless abandon. The following is a list of things to do to help make your pursuit practical:

1. Prayer...

2. Study...

3. Read...

4. Laying on of hands...

5. Associations...

6. Obedience...

Jesus said, "As the Father sent Me, I also send you." He did the works of the Father, and then passed the baton on to us.

(Quote From *When Heaven Invades Earth,* Pages 101-104)

QUESTIONS

1. Bringing the Father's heart to the world is quite a mission statement! How best would you be able to do this? What would be your first priority? Second? Third?

2. Imagine a bull's-eye in a heart shape painted on each person you have the opportunity to speak to during your day. Who would be the most difficult to target? Who would be easiest? Who might repel your love when you give it? How will you respond, whether the love is received or not?

3. Are you called to express the Father's love to a specific group of people or within a certain ministry? Is the love of God your motivation for what you do, or is there another agenda? Check your heart and be sure you are truly doing what the Father's will is.

4. Consciously taking God with us everywhere we go takes preparation and spontaneous focus. What do you think the preparation might entail? How can you remind yourself to be constantly aware of the Lord's Kingdom throughout your conversations and work?

5. Look at the list of six items that the author has given to help make your pursuit practical. Rate yourself on each one on a scale of 1-10 with 10 being the highest. Where do you need to improve? What steps will you take to do so?

6. When Jesus passed the baton to us, He literally sent us to do what He did. That means we are to continue the race with the same attitude, obedience, substance, and power. How do you think the Church can do this and successfully win the race? How will we know victory is achieved?

MEDITATION

*"We are the carriers of His presence, doers
of His will. Giving what we have received releases
Him into situations previously held in the grip
of darkness. That is our responsibility and privilege"*
(*When Heaven Invades Earth*, Page 101).

*Let the Lord "knight" you into His special
service today. Spend time in prayer preparing
to accomplish great exploits for His Kingdom.*

Powerlessness:
Unnecessary and Unbalanced

Heal the sick, cleanse the lepers, raise the dead, cast out demons. Freely you have received, freely give (Matthew 10:8).

While character must be at the heart of our ministries, power revolutionizes the world around us. Until the Church returns to Jesus' model for true revolutionaries, we will continue to be recognized by the world merely as nice people—while it is overcome with disease and torment, on its way to hell.

Some Christians actually have considered it to be more noble to choose *character* over *power*. But we must not separate the two. It is an unjustifiable, illegitimate choice. Together they bring us to the only real issue—obedience.

Once, while teaching a group of students about the importance of signs and wonders in the ministry of the gospel, a young man spoke up saying, "I'll pursue signs and wonders when I know I have more of the character of Christ in me." As good as that may sound, it comes from a religious mind-set, not a heart abandoned to the gospel of Jesus Christ. In response to this student's comment, I opened to the Gospel of Matthew and read the Lord's charge: "Go therefore and make disciples of all nations...teaching them to observe all things that I have commanded you" (Mt. 28:19). I then asked him, "Who gave you the right to determine when you are ready to obey His command?"

(Quote From *When Heaven Invades Earth*, Page 107)

QUESTIONS

1. In your own words, explain the place character has in ministry. Why has the character of well-known evangelists and preachers been at the center of controversies? How should we pray for those who have risen to prominence?

2. How does "power revolutionize the world around us"? What testimony does power make to the lost of the world? As a revolutionary of the Lord Jesus, where is your power? Is it demonstrating itself regularly? Does it leave a testimony wherever you go?

3. If you had to choose between character or power, which would you choose? Why? Why is this an unjustifiable, illegitimate choice? Why do we need both of these to obey?

4. Why do those who want character *before* signs and wonders build a religious mind-set in themselves? What makes a heart abandoned to the gospel of Jesus Christ?

5. Because the Lord is our Commander, we don't choose when we will obey. That means we might not think we are ready when He asks us, but we must obey anyway. Is this a step of faith? What makes us choose obedience over the questions in our minds?

6. Make a list of the Christians who are prominent in your world. Some may be local, some national. Pray each day this week for them to have the character to back up a ministry marked by power.

❊ MEDITATION ❊

*"Many believers have made it their primary
goal in life to be well-respected citizens of their
communities. Good character enables us to
be solid contributors to society, but most of what
is recognized as a Christian lifestyle can be
accomplished by people who don't even know God.
Every believer should be highly respected AND
MORE. It's the and more part that we're often lacking"*
(*When Heaven Invades Earth*, Page 107).

*Take some time to consider what you
are lacking. How could God use you
if you were highly respected AND MORE?*

Clothed With Power

A ND SUDDENLY THERE CAME A SOUND FROM HEAVEN, AS OF A RUSHING MIGHTY WIND, AND IT FILLED THE WHOLE HOUSE WHERE THEY WERE SITTING (ACTS 2:2).

So great was the disciples need for power to become witnesses that they were not to leave Jerusalem until they had it. That word *power, dunamis,* speaks of the miracle realm. It comes from dunamai, which means "ability." Think about it—we get to be clothed with *God's ability*!

The remaining eleven disciples were already the most trained people in signs and wonders in all of history....And it was those eleven who had to stay until they were clothed with *power from on high.* When they got it they knew it. This power came through an encounter with God.

Some, because of their fear of error, have said it's improper to seek for an experience with God. After all, many deceived groups have come from those who based their beliefs on experiences in conflict with Scripture. Under the guidance of such attitudes, fear becomes our teacher. But why aren't those same individuals afraid of belonging to the doctrinally stable camps that are powerless? Is this deception any less dangerous than that of the power abuser? Will you bury your gifts and tell the Master when He comes that you were afraid of being wrong? Power and character are so closely aligned in Scripture that you cannot be weak in one without undermining the other.

(Quote From *When Heaven Invades Earth,* Page 111)

QUESTIONS

1. The disciples needed power even though they had firsthand training from an incarnate Jesus. What kind of power do you think we need? From where do we get our firsthand training? What kind of training is necessary to help us become witnesses?

2. Consider for a moment the concept of you being clothed with God's ability. What does this mean in terms of potential? What does this mean in terms of responsibility?

3. The disciples received their power in a most dramatic way in Acts 2. Do you think people receive power this dramatically with every encounter of God? Why or why not? What do you think should accompany all encounters with God?

4. What is "fear of error"? Are you familiar with any error in beliefs concerning the power of God? How can we be sure we don't fall into error? Are there principles from the Word that help guide us? What are they?

5. Do you know of groups who have doctrinal stability but are powerless? What are these groups afraid of? How can we be sure we don't become powerless?

6. In your understanding, how can you become balanced in using your gifts freely, yet not abusing them? In what ways are character and power aligned in Scripture? How do these help safeguard each other?

MEDITATION

"If [God] is to be free to move in our
lives, we will constantly be involved in
impossibilities. The supernatural is His natural
realm. The more important the Holy Spirit becomes to
us, the more these issues will be paramount in our hearts"
(*When Heaven Invades Earth*, Page 112).

How natural is the supernatural in your life?
Does God bring you lots of impossibilities so
that you can overcome them and bear testimony to His
*power? How well do you **flow** with the Holy Spirit?*

Prayer—The Gateway to Power

F OR CHRIST DID NOT SEND ME TO BAPTIZE, BUT TO PREACH THE GOSPEL—NOT WITH WORDS OF HUMAN WISDOM, LEST THE CROSS OF CHRIST BE EMPTIED OF ITS POWER (1 CORINTHIANS 1:17 NIV).

❧ TODAY'S DEVOTION ❧

*J*esus said that we must receive the Kingdom like a child. The life of power is at home in the heart of a child. A child has an insatiable appetite to learn. Be childlike and read the works of those who have succeeded in the healing ministry....We have grown fat on the theories of classroom Christians. We must learn from those who *just do it!*...

If we teach, preach, or witness and nothing happens, we must go back to the drawing board—our knees. Do not make excuses for powerlessness. For decades the Church has been guilty of creating doctrine to justify their lack of power, instead of crying out to God until He changed them. The lie they came to believe has given rise to an entire branch of theology that has infected the Body of Christ with a fear of the Holy Spirit. It deceives under the guise of staying undeceived. The Word must go forth with power. Power is the realm of the Spirit. A powerless Word is *the letter* not *the Spirit*. And we all know, "The letter kills, but the Spirit gives life" (2 Cor. 3:6). Lives must be changed in our ministry of the Word. Keep in mind that conversion is the greatest and most precious miracle of all.

(Quote From *When Heaven Invades Earth,* Pages 115-116)

QUESTIONS

1. What do you think Jesus meant when He said we must receive the Kingdom like a child? Are we to be innocent? Are we to be cute? What does He really expect from an adult who would receive the Kingdom like a child?

2. Are you a learner? Do you have an insatiable appetite to learn? Do you have a teachable spirit? Do you have the humility to be taught by those God chooses to instruct you?

3. Who are the people you know who have successful healing ministries? If you don't know any, ask your pastor or someone you respect to recommend people, books, or tapes for your instruction. Be sure these people do not just talk about healing as a theory but actually see healing miracles in their ministry.

4. When you fail at teaching, preaching, or witnessing, do you quickly go to your knees in prayer? Have you ever rationalized why your words had no effect? What do these self-justifications do to keep you from the real Source of power?

5. When you believe your own rationalizations, you believe a lie. How do you break through the lies that build up in your life and wake up to what really is wrong? Why do you think crying out to God banishes pride from your life? How can God change your mind-set?

6. Why do you think many people are fearful of the Holy Spirit? Why do many find it easier to follow the letter of the law and not the Spirit of the law? Why is change so disconcerting to many people? Is there an issue of control? Are there any other issues at work here?

MEDITATION

"We hear a lot about what the anointing costs. Without question, walking with God in power will cost all who give themselves to this mandate. But the absence of power is even more costly" (*When Heaven Invades Earth*, Page 117).

Has the absence of power personally cost you anything? Has it hurt your ministry or witness? What price do you need to pay to receive power from on high?

The High Cost of Low Power

IF I HAD NOT DONE AMONG THEM THE WORKS WHICH NO ONE ELSE DID, THEY WOULD HAVE NO SIN; BUT NOW THEY HAVE SEEN AND ALSO HATED BOTH ME AND MY FATHER (JOHN 15:24).

❧ TODAY'S DEVOTION ❧

*R*evival is the atmosphere in which Christ's power is most likely to be manifested. It touches every part of human life, breaking into society with sparks of revolution. Such glory is costly, and it is not to be taken lightly. Nevertheless, a powerless Church is far more costly in terms of human suffering and lost souls. During revival, hell is plundered and heaven is populated. Without revival, hell is populated...period.

Let me illustrate the necessity of signs and wonders in our quest to see our cities transformed and the glory of God fill the earth. Without [them], the world suffers, God is grieved, and we are the most to be pitied....

A primary purpose of the miracle realm is to reveal the nature of God. The lack of miracles works like a thief, stealing precious revelation that is within the grasp of every man, woman, and child. Our debt to mankind is to give them answers for the impossible, and a personal encounter with God. And that encounter must include great power.

We are to be a witness for God. To give *witness* is to "represent." This actually means to *re-present* Him. Therefore, to re-present Him without power is a major shortcoming. It is impossible to give an adequate witness of God without demonstrating His supernatural power.

(Quote From *When Heaven Invades Earth,* Page 119)

QUESTIONS

1. Give a description of what you think "revival" is. What are its components? How do you know that it is truly revival? Have you ever experienced revival? What was involved? What kind of revolution does it spark?

2. What is the cost of revival and the accompanying glory? Do you think most Christians are willing to pay the price? Why or why not?

3. How do signs and wonders help transform cities? How do they usher in the glory of God? Have you seen a community impacted by miracles? How could this happen?

4. How does the lack of signs and wonders make the world suffer? How does this lack grieve God? Have you experienced any of these negative repercussions?

5. Explain how miracles reveal the nature of God. Do they make God more real to you? If so, in what way? What part of God's character becomes real through seeing the miraculous?

6. How are miracles a witness of God and His Kingdom? In what ways do they represent Him? If there is no power accompanying our words, how do we have an inadequate witness?

MEDITATION

*"Power exposes sin and brings people
to a decision. When power is missing, we are
not using the weapons that were in Jesus' arsenal
when He ministered to the lost. The outcome?
Most remain lost. Power forces people to be aware
of God on a personal level, and it is demanding in nature"*
(*When Heaven Invades Earth*, Page 121).

*Has the power of God ever exposed sin
in your life? Did it bring you to a decision? Describe
the demand that power puts on the life of a believer.*

Miracles Reveal His Glory

THIS BEGINNING OF SIGNS JESUS DID IN CANA OF GALILEE, AND MANIFESTED HIS GLORY; AND HIS DISCIPLES BELIEVED IN HIM (JOHN 2:11).

❧ TODAY'S DEVOTION ❧

*J*esus attended a wedding where they ran out of wine. As yet He hadn't performed any of the wonders for which He would later become known. Mary knew who her son was and what was possible....Her faith just made room for the extravagance of God! Jesus followed this with the miracle of turning the water into wine....

Jesus again looked to see what the Father was doing and now noticed that He was turning water into wine. So Jesus followed His lead and did the miracle. [Mary's] faith so touched the heart of the Father that He apparently changed the chosen time to unveil Jesus as the miracle worker. Faith moves heaven, so that heaven will move earth.

According to John 2:11, this demonstration of God's power released the glory of God into that location. Signs and wonders do that. They release the glory of God into our cities. The need—be it physical sickness, poverty, oppression, etc.—represents the impact of darkness. The miracle displaces darkness and replaces it with light—glory. When miracles are absent, so is the glory of God, which is the manifested presence of Jesus.

(Quote From *When Heaven Invades Earth*, Pages 123-124)

QUESTIONS

1. The first known miracle that Jesus performed was changing water into wine. Would it have been your choice for how Jesus would usher in His supernatural ministry? Are our misconceptions often blocks to participation in the miraculous?

2. How did Mary's faith change whether a miracle would be performed that day or not? Do you think she had seen other miracles and knew He was able to perform them? What kind of evidence do you need in order for your faith to engage?

3. How easy is it for you to tap and see what the Father is doing? What blocks your view? What enables it? How strong is your faith in this area?

4. The author tells us, "Faith moves heaven, so that heaven will move earth." Why is this true? How does this happen? Is God changing His mind when we exercise faith? Why or why not?

5. The miracle at the wedding ushered a season of power in Cana. Why do you think this happened? What kind of effect do you think it had on the citizens? On the local government? On the social welfare of the people?

6. From your answers to the questions in #5, draw some conclusions as to what changes might occur if miracles took place in your church this Sunday. How would it affect your community?

❊ MEDITATION ❊

"How will the glory of God cover the earth?
I believe that, at least in part, it will be
through a people who walk in power, bringing
the testimony of Jesus to the nations of the
world. There will be a generation that will catch
this and will invade the world system with
this living testimony of who Jesus is!"
(*When Heaven Invades Earth*, Page 124).

How determined are you to be part of the
testimony that will bring the glory of God?
Have you caught the vision of walking in power?
Will you commit to being part of heaven's
invasion on earth by being a living testimony?

How Do We Get the Power?

B EHOLD, I SEND THE PROMISE OF MY
FATHER UPON YOU; BUT TARRY IN THE
CITY OF JERUSALEM UNTIL YOU ARE ENDUED
WITH POWER FROM ON HIGH (LUKE 24:49).

*J*esus commanded the most highly trained individuals in the supernatural to ever walk the earth to "wait in Jerusalem for what the Father has promised " (Acts 1:4)....The baptism of fire would give them their own ongoing encounter that would help to keep them at the center of God's will *when* persecution came.

The baptism of the Holy Spirit is an immersion into the *dunamis* of heaven. The ability to pray in tongues is a wonderful gift given through this baptism. I pray in tongues constantly, and am grateful for such a gift from God. But to think that speaking in tongues is *the* purpose for such a holy invasion is embarrassingly simplistic. It would be the same as saying that when Israel crossed the Jordan River it was the same as possessing the Promised Land. Yes, they were in it, they could see it, but they did not possess it! Their river crossing gave them the legal access to the possession. This wonderful Spirit baptism has given us such an access. But to stand on the banks proclaiming *it's all mine*, is foolishness at best. Such ignorance has caused great numbers of people to halt their pursuit once they've received their spiritual language. They have been taught they are now full of the Holy Spirit.

(Quote From *When Heaven Invades Earth*, Pages 128-129)

QUESTIONS

1. Do you like it when you are told to "wait"? Why or why not. When Jesus asked the disciples to "wait," what test did the disciples face? Did they understand what the Father had promised...in other words, did they know what they were waiting for? What spiritual empowerment are you waiting for?

2. What is an "ongoing encounter"? How did the disciples' baptism create this? Have you had a baptism of fire? If so, has it empowered an "ongoing encounter"?

3. How does an "ongoing encounter" with God help to keep a person in the center of God's will when persecution comes? Why is this so crucial to our ongoing witness and impact on the world?

4. How are the ability to pray in tongues and *dunamis* interconnected? What do you think the purpose of speaking in tongues is?

5. Spirit baptism gives us access to what? Describe what we receive immediately and what we receive when we continue to grow in *dunamis*.

6. What are to be our pursuits after the baptism of the Holy Spirit? What must we do to gain our pursuits? How do we know if we are growing in these or not?

❧ MEDITATION ❧

"A glass is only full when it overflows.
Fullness can only be measured by overflow.
The fullness of God ought to do more for me than
give me a supernatural language. If that's all there
was, I'd have no complaint. It's a glorious gift from
God. But His purposes bring us into more, to a divine
partnership in which we become co-laborers with Christ"
(*When Heaven Invades Earth*, Page 129).

Are you full of God? Do you have
a regular overflow that is measurable? What
does your partnership with God look like?

Our Debt to the World: An Encounter With God

IF THE HOUSEHOLD IS WORTHY, LET YOUR PEACE COME UPON IT. BUT IF IT IS NOT WORTHY, LET YOUR PEACE RETURN TO YOU (MATTHEW 10:13).

God's covenant promise, "I will be with you," has always been linked to mankind's need for courage to face the impossible. There is no question that the presence of God is what brings us great comfort and peace. But the presence of God was always promised to His chosen ones to give them assurance in the face of less than favorable circumstances.

He is the great treasure of mankind. He always will be. It is this revelation that enabled the revolutionary exploits of the apostle Paul. It's what strengthened a king named David to risk his life in order to transform the system of sacrifice and worship. Moses needed this assurance as the man who was sent to face Pharaoh and his demon-possessed magicians. They all needed incredible confidence to fulfill their callings....

The Great Commission provides more interesting reading for those who remember what kind of men God was giving His charge to—greedy, prideful, angry, and self-centered. Yet Jesus called them to change the world. What was the one word of assurance that He gave them before departing from sight? "I will be with you always..." (see Mt. 28:19-21)....

The presence of God is to be realized in the anointing. Remember, anointing means *smeared*—it is God covering us with His power-filled presence. Supernatural things happen when we walk in the anointing!

(Quote From *When Heaven Invades Earth*, Pages 133-134)

QUESTIONS

1. What is the connection between the presence of God and peace? How does this work? What is your peace like—intermittent or constant? How does your answer reflect the presence of God in your life?

2. What is the true test as to whether you have peace or not? When unfavorable circumstances enter your life, does peace reign? When you are faced with challenges, what emotions can rise to the surface that are not God's choice? What are the negative thoughts that may come?

3. How did you come to discover that God is the great treasure of your life? Has this revelation made a difference in how you live each day? Have you done any revolutionary exploits that resemble Paul's? Have you received strength and helped transform anything within the Church? Have you received assistance to face opposition square in the face?

4. What kind of confidence does the presence of God bring? Do you find that you are more confident than a year ago? Why or why not? How does confidence grow within us?

5. If Jesus was not uncomfortable trusting His disciples with the job of changing the world, do you think He is uncomfortable trusting you with your commission? Truthfully, do you believe Jesus can overcome your shortcomings and still use you to do His Kingdom work?

6. Describe what the "anointing" is to you. If the "presence of God is to be realized in the anointing," how does your description come to bear on the presence of God? Describe what being "smeared" by God means to you. How does this smearing affect your daily life?

❧ MEDITATION ❧

*"Why do some walk with a greater sense
of God's presence than others? Some people
place high value on the presence of God, and
others don't. The ones who do enjoy fellowship
throughout their day with the Holy Spirit are
extremely conscious of how He feels about their words,
attitudes, and activities. The thought of grieving Him
brings great sorrow. It's their passion to give Him
preeminence in everything. That passion brings that
believer into a supernatural life—one with the constant
activity of the Holy Spirit working through them"*
(*When Heaven Invades Earth*, Page 134).

*Reflect on which of these sentences describe you
and which do not. Where do you want to go from here?*

Jesus Passed the Baton

Most assuredly, I say to you, he who believes in Me, the works that I do he will do also; and greater works than these he will do, because I go to My Father (John 14:12).

*F*or us to become all that God intended, we must remember that Jesus' life was a model of what mankind could become if it were in right relationship with the Father. Through the shedding of His blood, it would be possible for everyone who believed on His name to do as He did and become as He was. This meant then that every true believer would have access to the realm of life that Jesus lived in.

Jesus came as the light of the world. He then passed the baton to us announcing that we are the light of the world. Jesus came as the miracle worker. He said that we would do "greater works" than He did (Jn. 14:12). He then pulled the greatest surprise of all, saying, "right now the Holy Spirit is with you, but He's going to be in you"(see Jn. 14:17). Jesus, who illustrates to us what is possible for those who are *right with God,* now says that His people are to be the tabernacle of God on planet earth. Paul affirms this revelation with statements such as, "Do you not know that you are the temple of God?" (1 Cor. 3:16) "…and you are a dwelling place of God" (Eph. 2:22).

(Quote From *When Heaven Invades Earth,* Page 138)

QUESTIONS

1. As you look at the life of Jesus, what are the striking aspects of His relationship with His Father that inspire you? List the results of the relationship between Jesus and His Father that speak most to you. Based on your answers, what would be the next steps toward a more intimate relationship with the Father?

2. Jesus is our model of Kingdom expansion. How does belief in His name bear weight on how much we become like Him? Describe the realm of life that is then open to us as believers.

3. Just as Jesus was the light of the world, we are to be the same. To be the light of the world, what would be your mission statement? What is your strategy to be the light wherever you go?

4. Just as Jesus was the miracle worker, we are to do greater miracles than He did. How is this possible? What kind of grade would you give the contemporary Church in doing greater things than Jesus did? Explain why you graded the Church the way you did.

5. After Jesus ascended, the Holy Spirit changed positions. Instead of being "with" us, He now is "in" us. Explain the difference between "with" and "in" in terms of the process, the results, and the relationship.

6. Trace the place where God has dwelled on earth: Moses' tabernacle...David's tabernacle...the temple in Jerusalem...our bodies. How does each dwelling place show the plan of God's relationship to man?

MEDITATION

*"What was the initial revelation of the
house of God? It has the presence of God,
a gate to heaven, and a ladder with angels
ascending and descending upon it. Why is this
important to understand? This revelation shows
the resources that are at our disposal to carry
out the Master's plan. This principle of being the
stewards of the heavenly realm then becomes more
than the assignment of the individual, and becomes the
privilege of an entire Church for the sake of their entire city"*
(*When Heaven Invades Earth*, Page 138).

*How does the understanding that you
have all of God's resources at your disposal make
you feel? Because they are to be used to carry out the
Master's plan, how is your stewardship vital? How does
your personal assignment affect your local church's assignment?*

Entering the Twilight Zone

Bless the Lord, you His angels, who excel in strength, who do His word, heeding the voice of His word (Psalm 103:20).

I travel to many cities that are spiritually very dark. When you enter such cities you can feel the oppression. Considering what I represent to that city, it would be wrong for me to focus on the darkness. I don't ever want to be impressed with the devil's work. I come as a *house of God*. As such I contain a gate to heaven, with a ladder providing angelic activities according to the need of the moment. Simply put, *I am an open heaven!* This does not apply to a select few. On the contrary, this revelation is about the house of God and the principles of the house apply to all believers. But few realize or implement this *potential* blessing. With an open heaven I become a vehicle in the hand of God to release the resources of heaven into the calamities of mankind. Angels are commissioned to carry out the will of God. "Bless the Lord, you His angels, who excel in strength, who do His word, heeding the voice of His word" (Ps. 103:20). He is more eager to invade this world than we are to receive the invasion. And angels play an integral part.

They respond to His command and enforce His Word. But the *voice of His word* is heard when the Father speaks to the hearts of His people.

(Quote From *When Heaven Invades Earth,* Page 140)

QUESTIONS

1. The author relays how he travels to cities that are spiritually dark. How would he feel the oppression he speaks of? Have you ever felt oppression? Did it overwhelm you or keep you from a strong spiritual connection?

2. Why do you think the author tells us that it would have been wrong for him to focus on darkness when he felt oppression? How can it deter us from great works that the Lord wants to do? Are you able to overcome darkness? How?

3. As a gate to heaven, you have authority to do what? Do you see yourself as someone who provides access to another dimension? How can people's needs be met in the spontaneity of the moment because of this open heaven?

4. How does God use you as a vehicle to release the resources of heaven into the calamities of mankind? Is this an issue of money only? What other resources are available to you? Is this confined to what you personally have, or are there other resources available?

5. Have you ever thought of God planning an "invasion" of planet earth? What factors would inhibit the invasion? Why aren't people ready to receive God's invasion?

6. Consider the statement, "The voice of His word is heard when the Father speaks to the hearts of His people." What does this mean to you? How does this voice speak to the angels? How does it release resources to earth?

❧ MEDITATION ❦

*"Angels await the people of God speaking
His word. I believe angels pick up the fragrance
of the throne room through the word spoken
by people. They can tell when a word has its
origins in the heart of the Father. And, in turn,
they recognize that word as their assignment"*
(*When Heaven Invades Earth*, Page 140).

*This is a beautiful portrayal of how
angels receive assignments. How is mankind
involved in this process? Is it weighty to
think of your connection with angelic assignments?*

Our Identity in This World

L OVE HAS BEEN PERFECTED AMONG US IN
THIS: THAT WE MAY HAVE BOLDNESS IN THE
DAY OF JUDGMENT; BECAUSE AS HE IS, SO ARE
WE IN THIS WORLD (1 JOHN 4:17).

While most of the Church is still trying to become as Jesus was, the Bible declares, "As He is, so are we in this world" (1 Jn. 4:17)....

The "as He is, so are we" declaration is far beyond what any of us could have imagined; especially in light of the glorified description of Jesus in Revelation, chapter 1. Yet, the Holy Spirit was sent specifically for this purpose that we might attain..."to the measure of the stature of the fullness of Christ" (Eph. 4:13).

The Holy Spirit came with the ultimate assignment at the perfect time. During Jesus' ministry, it was said, "The Holy Spirit was not yet given, because Jesus was not yet glorified (Jn. 7:39). The Holy Spirit comforts us, gives us gifts, reminds us of what Jesus has said, and clothes us with power. But He does all this to *make us like Jesus.* That is His primary mission. So why didn't the Father send Him until Jesus was glorified? Because without Jesus in His glorified state there was no *heavenly model of what we were to become!* As a sculptor looks at a model and fashions the clay into its likeness, so the Holy Spirit looks to the glorified Son and shapes us into His image. *As He is, so are we in this world.*

(Quote From *When Heaven Invades Earth,* Page 145)

QUESTIONS

1. Explain what you think First John 4:17 means to your life. How does the fact that Jesus is no longer incarnate impact what you are to become?

2. How does Jesus' glorified description in Revelation, chapter 1 impact you? List the verses that describe Him and make personal notes regarding each one.

3. What is the "stature of the fullness of Christ"? How do you "measure" up? What part of the fullness of Christ is easily seen in your life? How does this measure testify to God's glory?

4. What is the true mission of the Holy Spirit in our lives? What is His strategy? What tools does He use to accomplish His mission? How is this possible?

5. If the Holy Spirit is as a sculptor and we are as the clay, how moldable and pliable are you in the hands of the Master Potter? Do you fashion easily into the shape He desires, or do you resist? Perhaps there are specific areas of more resistance than others. If so, what are they? What might you do to become more pliable?

6. How can you be more like Jesus to this world? Because many are looking for something other than the glorified Christ, you will need to think in terms outside this world. How will you take on a Jesus model and move in power and authority?

❈ MEDITATION ❈

*"Jesus became poor so that I could
become rich. He suffered with stripes to free me
from affliction, and He became sin so I might
become the righteousness of God (see 2 Cor. 5:21).
Why then should I try to become **as He was**,
when He suffered so I could become **as He is**?
At some point, the reality of the resurrection must
come into play in our lives—we must discover the power
of the resurrection for all who believe (see Eph. 1:21; 3:20)"*
(*When Heaven Invades Earth*, Page 146).

*Consider why you should become as He is.
Is the resurrection an everyday consideration in your life?*

Becoming Like Him

✦

THEN MARY SAID, "BEHOLD THE MAIDSER-
VANT OF THE LORD! LET IT BE TO ME
ACCORDING TO YOUR WORD." AND THE ANGEL
DEPARTED FROM HER (LUKE 1:38).

✦

A s He is, so are we in this world. The revelation of Jesus in His glorified state has at least four overwhelming characteristics that directly affect the coming transformation of the Church; these must be embraced as a part of God's plan in these final hours.

Glory—This is the manifested presence of Jesus....He lives in all believers, but the glory of His presence comes to rest on only a few. It is sometimes seen and frequently felt. He is returning for a glorious Church. It is not an option....

Power—To be *as He is* involves being a continuous expression of power. The baptism in the Holy Spirit clothes us with this heavenly element....It is the *power of salvation*—for the body, soul, and spirit....

Triumph—Jesus conquered all things: the power of hell, the grave, sin, and the devil....Every name and power has been placed under His feet. He calls us His body—and this body has feet....This victory doesn't mean we live without battles; it simply means our victory is secured....

Holiness—Jesus is perfectly holy—separate *from* all that is evil, *unto* all that is good. Holiness is the language through which the nature of God is revealed....Holiness in the Church reveals the beauty of God.

(Quote From *When Heaven Invades Earth*, Pages 149-150)

QUESTIONS

1. Mary believed the angel and then lived out her assignment. It was that simple...or was it? Trace the difficulties Mary faced in those months and years after the angelic visitation. She had to continuously go back to the reality of the visitation and remind herself of her assignment. What is your assignment? What difficulties have you faced that force you to revisit your call to it?

2. In your opinion, how does *glory* directly affect the coming transformation of the Church? How does it affect your transformation?

3. In your opinion, how does *power* directly affect the coming transformation of the Church? How does it affect your transformation?

4. In your opinion, how does *triumph* directly affect the coming transformation of the Church? How does it affect your transformation?

5. In your opinion, how does *holiness* directly affect the coming transformation of the Church? How does it affect your transformation?

6. Summarize how these four overwhelming characteristics affect the Church as a whole in terms of its transformation. Then summarize how the total impact of the above four characteristics impact your own transformation.

❊ MEDITATION ❊

*"At some point we must rise up to the
high call of God and stop saying things about
ourselves that are no longer true. If we're going
to fully come in to what God has for us in this
last days' revival, we will have to come to grips
with the issue of being more than **sinners saved by
grace**. Maturity comes from faith in the sufficiency
of God's redemptive work that establishes us
as sons and daughters of the Most High"*
(*When Heaven Invades Earth*, Page 149).

*How can we see ourselves as not just
sinners saved by grace but heirs of God?
What does it take for us to believe we are
precious in God's sight even when we don't feel it?*

Warring to Invade!

To execute on them the written judgment—this honor have all His saints (Psalm 149:9).

---

*F*or too long the Church has played defense in the battle for souls....This may come as a surprise, but I don't care what the devil plans to do. The Great Commission puts me on the offensive. I've got the ball. And if I carry the ball effectively, his plans won't matter....

Spiritual warfare is unavoidable, and ignoring this subject won't make it go away. Therefore, we must learn to battle with supernatural authority! The following principles are often overlooked insights:...

1. The safest place in this war is obedience....

2. Never allow anything to distract you from this point of strength....

3. When we refuse fear, the enemy becomes terrified....

4. Submission is the key to personal triumph....

5. The Church is on the attack. That's why...the *gates of hell,* the place of demonic government and strength, **WILL NOT PREVAIL** against the Church....

6. It is His delight to have us enforce the triumph of Jesus....

7. Praise honors God. But it also edifies us and destroys the powers of hell!...

This is by no means a complete list. It's just enough to turn our perspective of spiritual warfare from one that is religious and carnal, to one that has a Kingdom mind-set.

(Quote From *When Heaven Invades Earth,* Pages 153-156)

QUESTIONS

1. Why do you think the Church has been on the defense and not on the offense in the battle for souls? Do you think the Church has focused on what the devil's plans are versus what God's are? What needs to change?

2. To be on the offensive means that we attack first...right? How do we know where to attack? What to attack? How to attack? With what weapons? How do we get our military strategy?

3. What do you think it means to "battle with supernatural authority"? How can we learn how to do this?

4. Look over the list of seven principles the author shares. Comment on each one in terms of your experience and ability in each area.

5. Look over the list again and find Scriptures that will help you gain strength in each.

6. Finally, make a point to memorize your Scriptures over the next seven weeks so that you are ready to pursue the enemy instead of allowing the enemy to pursue you.

MEDITATION

*"We were born in a war. There are no
time-outs, no vacations, no leaves of absence.
The safest place is in the center of God's will,
which is the place of deep intimacy. There He
allows only the battles to come our way
that we are equipped to win"*
(*When Heaven Invades Earth*, Page 156).

*Even though war is inevitable, how
comforting it is to know we can win every
one. How is this possible? Is it probable?*

How to Miss a Revival

❖

FOR THE HEARTS OF THIS PEOPLE HAVE GROWN DULL. THEIR EARS ARE HARD OF HEARING, AND THEIR EYES THEY HAVE CLOSED, LEST THEY SHOULD SEE WITH THEIR EYES AND HEAR WITH THEIR EARS, LEST THEY SHOULD UNDERSTAND WITH THEIR HEARTS AND TURN, SO THAT I SHOULD HEAL THEM (MATTHEW 13:15).

❖

*H*istory is filled with people who prayed for a visitation of God and missed it when it came. And this happened even though some had a strong relationship with God.

Many believers have a blindness that the world doesn't have. The world knows its need. But for many Christians, once they are born again they gradually stop recognizing their need. There is something about desperation for God that enables a person to recognize whether or not something is from God. Jesus spoke of this phenomenon saying, "For judgment I have come into this world, that those who do not see may see, and that those who see may be made blind" (Jn. 9:39).

The testimony of history and the record of Scripture warn us of the possibility of this error. "Therefore let him who thinks he stands take heed lest he fall" (1 Cor. 10:12). Matthew says it's the dull of heart who can't see (see Mt. 13:15). A dull knife is one that has been used. The implication is that the *dull of heart* had a history in God, but did not keep current in what God was doing. We maintain our *sharp edge* as we recognize our need and passionately pursue Jesus. This *first love* somehow keeps us safely in the center of God's activities on earth.

(Quote From *When Heaven Invades Earth*, Pages 157-158)

QUESTIONS

1. Why do you think so many have missed a visitation from God after they had spent time on their knees praying for it? Doesn't a strong relationship with God prevent such things? Why or why not?

2. Why do you think "recognizing our need" is so important to the believer? How desperate are you for God?

3. Explain the meaning of John 9:39. Who do the "blind" refer to here? Who are the ones who can see? Why did Jesus say such things?

4. In First Corinthians 10:12, it speaks about a person "who thinks he stands." What does this mean? A person of this description might have fallen prey to what types of sins? How do you think you can avoid these sins?

5. What does "dull of heart" mean? Why does this condition prevent spiritual sight? How can someone keep "current" with what God is doing? Is this a current events exercise or something else?

6. How sharp is your edge? How do you fan the flame of your first love? What part of your relationship with God may need some fanning currently?

❧ MEDITATION ❧

*"Revival is central to the message of the
Kingdom, for it is in revival that we more clearly
see what His dominion looks like and how it is to
affect society. Revival at its best is, Thy Kingdom come.
In a way, revival illustrates the normal Christian life"*
(*When Heaven Invades Earth*, Page 157).

*Have you ever read about past revivals?
Research the Internet or read a book that
describes some of the greatest revivals and the
people who preached during them. Consider
what they preached and apply it to today's world.*

Close Encounters

NOW TO HIM WHO IS ABLE TO DO EXCEED-
INGLY ABUNDANTLY ABOVE ALL THAT WE
ASK OR THINK, ACCORDING TO THE POWER
THAT WORKS IN US (EPHESIANS 3:20).

*T*hink about the Acts 2 experience of the disciples. Notice the elements of this Spirit-directed service:

1. They were praying.

2. They were in unity.

3. They all spoke in tongues.

4. Unbelievers heard those tongues.

5. People were saved.

Consider the Acts 2 company's predicament: they just had an encounter with God without a chapter and verse to explain what just happened. Peter, under the direction of the Holy Spirit, chose to use Joel 2 as the proof-text to give the needed backbone to their experience. Joel 2 declares there would be an outpouring of the Holy Spirit involving prophecy, dreams, and visions. The outpouring happened as promised in Acts 2, but it had none of the things mentioned by Joel. Instead it had the sound of wind, fire, and tongues. It was God who used this passage to support this new experience.

The very fact that this seems like an improper interpretation of Scripture should reveal to us that it is we who often approach His book incorrectly. The Bible is not a book of lists that confine or corral God. The Word does not contain God—it reveals Him. Joel 2 revealed the nature of God's work among man. Acts 2 was an illustration of what God intended by that prophecy.

(Quote From *When Heaven Invades Earth,* Pages 162-163)

QUESTIONS

1. Look at the five elements of the Spirit-directed service in Acts 2. How many of these depict your local church? Should this happen each and every worship service? Why or why not? Is there a system we are to employ, or will each Spirit-led service have differences?

2. If you had been one of the disciples and experienced the outpouring of Acts 2, how would you have reacted? Would an explanation be necessary to you right then and there? Why or why not? Would believers need an explanation later to understand what had happened? Why or why not?

3. Read Joel 2: 28-29. Look at the people groups mentioned here. Why were each used as examples of where God would pour out His Spirit? Does this help validate the ones He chose to use in Acts 2? Does this help validate why He would choose you and your local church? How?

4. What is the difference between confining or corralling God and explaining what God does? Where do you cross the line between these two? What do we have to avoid when we give explanation for how God is working?

5. The link between Joel and Acts provides an example of how the Old and New Testaments work together to bring principles of God's Word to us. Explain how this is true with these two passages. Are there others you can cite that are not exact quotes of each other but help clarify how the Lord works? If so, give examples.

6. "The Word does not contain God—it reveals Him." What does this mean to you? How does this give room to experience God each time you read the Word?

❧ MEDITATION ❧

*"We miss God when we live as though
we have Him figured out. We have the habit
of making Him look like us. In fact, if we think
we understand Him we have probably conformed
Him into our image. There must remain mystery
in our relationship with this One who has
purposed to work beyond our capacity to
imagine. To endeavor to know Him is to embark
on an adventure in which questions increase"*
(*When Heaven Invades Earth*, Page 164).

*Think about your relationship with God.
Is there mystery involved in it? Do you see
your relationship as an adventure? Do questions
increase because of your growing intimacy?*

Infiltrating the System

AND again He said, "To what shall I liken the kingdom of God? It is like leaven, which a woman took and hid in three measures of meal till it was all leavened" (Luke 13:20-21).

Without a revelation of what God intends to do with His Church, we cannot move in overcoming faith. When the main goal of our faith is keeping us safe from the devil, our faith becomes inferior to what God expects. Jesus had in mind more for us than survival. We are destined to overcome.

Every conversion plunders hell. Every miracle destroys the works of the devil. Every God encounter is an *Invasion of the Almighty* into our desperate condition. This is our joy.

The original flame of Pentecost, the Holy Spirit Himself, burns within my soul. I have a promise from God. I am a part of a company of people destined to do greater works than Jesus did in His earthly ministry. Why is it so hard to see the Church with significant influence in the last days? It was God who determined that the bride should be spotless and without wrinkle. It was God who declared, "Behold darkness will cover the earth, but His glory will appear upon you" (Isa. 60:2 NAS). It was God who calls us, His Church, overcomers (see Rev. 12:11).

The parable about leaven illustrates the subtle but overwhelming influence of the Kingdom in any setting into which it is placed. In these days, God has planned to put us into the darkest of situations to demonstrate His dominion.

(Quote From *When Heaven Invades Earth,* Page 166)

QUESTIONS

1. Why do we need a revelation of what God intends to do with His Church? What does this have to do with moving in overcoming faith?

2. How can the devil become a distraction to the direction of your faith? How easy is it to replace a mind-set of "survival" with a mind-set toward "overcoming"? Have you been able to do it? What do you think are the necessary steps to change anyone's mind-set?

3. Explain how conversions plunder hell and miracles destroy the works of the devil. If these are the military invasion strategy of God, why doesn't the Church have more success in the campaign? What part are you playing in this invasion?

4. The Church is supposed to be influential in the last days. Is it currently? Why or why not? What can improve its influence? What will the Church need to become involved in, to a greater capacity, for there to be effective influence?

5. Isaiah 60:2 says that God's glory will come upon us. How does this happen? How are you bringing God's glory into the darkness?

6. Instead of despairing over the darkness of the times, we are to see our opportunity to have greater influence. Why will this be true? Are you ready to negotiate the darkness in order to bring dominion? Why or why not?

❧ MEDITATION ❧

"A jeweler often places a diamond
on a piece of black velvet. The brilliance of
the gem is clearer against that background.
So it is with the Church. The dark
condition of world's circumstances becomes
the backdrop upon which He displays
His glorious Church! 'Where sin abounded,
grace abounded much more' (Rom. 5:20)"

(*When Heaven Invades Earth*, Page 166).

Think about your local church as a jewel
in your community of black velvet. How well
does it display God's glorious Church? What
do people think about your church in your
community? How is your church seen by
other churches? How can we help display our
local churches so that God's brilliance will be easily seen?

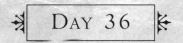

The Power of Holiness

A ND He said to them, "Go into all the
world and preach the gospel to
every creature" (Mark 16:15).

So much of today's Kingdom theology is focused on us ruling, in the sense of believers becoming the heads of corporations and governments. And, in measure, it is true. But our strong suit has been, and always will be, service. If in serving we get promoted to positions of rulership, we must remember that *what got us there, will keep us useful.* In the Kingdom, the greatest is the servant of all. Use every position to serve with more power....

Infiltrating the system often involves our willingness to bring spiritual gifts into our world. These gifts actually work better in the world than in the confines of church meetings. When we practice the gifts only in the church, they lose their sharp edge. Invading the world system with His dominion keeps us sharp and gets them saved....

The presence of the Kingdom saves the lives of people who have not earned it through personal obedience. Such is the power of righteousness—it protects those around it.

Promotion does not go unchallenged. Just when you think you have been placed into a position of influence, something will happen to totally rock your boat....There is a distinction between submission and obedience. Sometimes we are to go against the command of our leaders—but even then, only with submissive hearts.

(Quote From *When Heaven Invades Earth,* Pages 168-169)

QUESTIONS

1. In order to lead, what does the Lord ask us to do? In order to be the greatest, what does He tell us to be? In order to be the first, what does the Lord require? Are we not to be ambitious? What place does ambition have?

2. How does servant leadership work? What are its requirements? What are its results? Are their any promises of promotion?

3. How do you "serve with more power"? Consider this thought another way—how can you get more power to serve? Who are the people who look up to you either in the home, in ministry, or in the business world? Do they see you as a servant? Take some time to ask them to evaluate the quality of your servanthood.

4. Our spiritual gifts are not to be used within the four walls of the church; we are to take these to the marketplace. In what ways can you use spiritual gifts where you work or live? They do not have to be identified as spiritual gifts, but actually means of infiltrating the system. Have you ever used a spiritual gift in a "secular" environment that brought special insight or success?

5. If we serve where we are positioned, God uses the power of our righteousness. How can this serve the people who work or live with us? Can this power affect the financial status of the corporation or house where we serve? Can this power affect the work climate? Explain.

6. Have you received promotion in ministry or on the job and experienced an immediate attack that challenged it? What happened? Is there a way to challenge leaders and peers without throwing submission out the window? How can this be done?

MEDITATION

"For massive worldwide revival to reach
its dominating potential, it must be taken out
of the four walls of the church and launched into
*the **marketplace** (see Mk. 6:56). Quietly,*
powerfully, decisively invade through service; and
when you run into a person with an impossibility,
let him know the reality of heaven is within arm's reach!"
(*When Heaven Invades Earth*, Page 170).

How do you view your Great Commission?
Is it easy to be a witness? Does your
holiness find power readily available when needed?

Taking It to the Marketplace

Wherever He entered, into villages, cities, or the country, they laid the sick in the marketplaces, and begged Him that they might just touch the hem of His garment. And as many as touched Him were made well (Mark 6:56).

*A*ny gospel that doesn't work in the marketplace, doesn't work. Jesus invaded every realm of society. He went where people gathered. They became His focus, and He became theirs.

We see businessmen use the gifts of the Spirit to identify the needs of their co-workers and customers. A young teammate laid hands on the star running back of his high school football team after he had been knocked out of the game with a serious leg injury. After the running back was healed, he returned to the game acknowledging God had healed him!...

A ten-year-old asked her mom to take her to the mall so she could find sick people to pray for. Students set up a sign at their table at our local coffee shop. It says, *"Free Prayer."* People not only got prayer, they received a prophetic word that brought them to a greater awareness of God's love....

Skateboarders are touched by other skateboarders who look to bring them into an encounter with the God of all power. If people are there, we go there. Under the bridges, out in the vacant lots, we look for the homeless.

(Quote From *When Heaven Invades Earth,* Pages 172-173)

QUESTIONS

1. "Any gospel that doesn't work in the marketplace, doesn't work." What does this mean? Do you think this is true? Explain your answer.

2. Think through the strata of society that Jesus invaded. Name people from these different social groups who were changed by bumping elbows with Jesus. Are these people representative of society today? Are we to bump elbows with them as Jesus did?

3. Jesus was focused on the people who gathered around Him. He considered all their needs. What are the needs of the people who are gathered around you at home, in ministry, in the marketplace? What do you do about these needs? What did Jesus do?

4. As Jesus focused on the people around Him, they began to focus on Him. Who have you led to Christ? Do you help people focus on the Lord by your acts of prayer, generosity, or service on their behalf?

5. The author gives examples of Christians who made a difference to the people around them. Ask the Lord to reveal who is the next priority of focus in your ministry in the marketplace. Begin to pray consistently for that person and allow the Lord to reveal acts of service or generosity that you might be able to do that will bring focus to Jesus.

6. No matter what religion they believe or don't believe, people across the world recognize God's love. When they see Mother Theresa or missionary agencies provide care in critical moments, they are not afraid to receive a "bless you" from the one ministering to them. Is there someone in your sphere of influence who has a crisis that is in need of a miracle? From prayer for a miracle to acts of kindness, are you able to find a way to minister a "bless you" to them in their hour of need?

❦ MEDITATION ❦

*"Not only does Jesus care for the down
and outer, but He also loves the up and outer.
The wealthy are some of the most broken of our cities.
But we must not serve them for their money! They
are accustomed to people becoming friends to get
something from them....Where does life take you?
Go there in the anointing and watch the
impossibilities bow to the name Jesus"*
(*When Heaven Invades Earth*, Page 173).

*Think about what the author has said
here and consider the impossibilities
before you. Grab the anointing and watch
those impossibilities bow to the name of Jesus.*

This Present Revival

To the intent that now the manifold wisdom of God might be made known by the church to the principalities and powers in the heavenly places, according to the eternal purpose which He accomplished in Christ Jesus our Lord (EPHESIANS 3:10–11).

*U*nderstanding what is about to come is important, but not to equip us to plan and strategize more effectively. On the contrary, it's important to understand God's promise and purpose for the Church so that we might become dissatisfied—so that we will become desperate. Intercession from insatiable hunger moves the heart of God as nothing else can.

Revival is not for the faint of heart. It brings fear to the complacent because of the risks it requires. The fearful often work against the move of God—sometimes to their death—all the while thinking they are working for Him. Deception says that the changes brought about by revival contradict the faith of their fathers. As a result, the God-given ability to create withers into the laborious task of preserving. The fearful become curators of museums, instead of builders of the Kingdom.

Others are ready to risk all. The faith of their fathers is considered a worthy foundation to build upon. They have caught a glimpse of what could be and will settle for nothing less. Change is not a threat, but an adventure. Revelation increases, ideas multiply, and the stretch begins.

(Quote From *When Heaven Invades Earth,* Page 177)

QUESTIONS

Think on Ephesians 3:10-11 in terms of the following phrases:

1. Manifold wisdom of God.
2. Known by the church.
3. To the principalities and powers in the heavenly places.
4. Eternal purpose.
5. Which He accomplished in Christ Jesus.

For each phrase explain:

- What you think it means.

- What impact it has on the world.

- What potential it has for your community.

- What demand it has for your life.

- Why it requires faith and courage.

- What change will be needed of the participants.

❧ MEDITATION ❧

"What God has planned for the
Church in this hour is greater than our ability
to imagine and pray.... We must have the help
of the Holy Spirit to learn about these mysteries
of the Church and God's Kingdom. Without
Him we don't have enough insight even
to know what to ask for in prayer"
(*When Heaven Invades Earth*, Page 177).

Has God ever stirred your imagination
beyond your normal scope of thinking? Have
you ever felt like you were dreaming His dream and
making it yours? Spend time asking the Lord to share
His heart and desires with you so you might add
*your faith to the dream and watch it come **to life**!*

Glorious Church

THAT HE MIGHT PRESENT HER TO HIMSELF A GLORIOUS CHURCH, NOT HAVING SPOT OR WRINKLE OR ANY SUCH THING, BUT THAT SHE SHOULD BE HOLY AND WITHOUT BLEMISH (EPHESIANS 5:27).

Wisdom is to be displayed by us NOW! It is clear that God intends to teach the spirit realm about His wisdom through those made in His image—us....

The wisdom of God will again be seen in His people. The Church, which is presently despised, or at best ignored, will again be reverenced and admired....

Excellence is the high standard for what we do because of who we are. God is extravagant, but not wasteful. An excellent heart for God may appear to be wasteful to those on the outside....Excellence comes from viewing things from His perspective....

Creativity is not only seen in a full restoration of the arts, but is the nature of His people in finding new and better ways to do things....We must reveal who our Father is through creative expression....This anointing will also bring about new inventions, breakthroughs in medicine and science, and novel ideas for business and education....

Integrity is the expression of God's character seen in us. And that character is His holiness. Holiness is the essence of His nature. It is not something He does or doesn't do. It is who He is. It is the same for us. We are holy because the nature of God is in us.

(Quote From *When Heaven Invades Earth*, Pages 180-181)

QUESTIONS

1. Define what "wisdom" means to you. How does God's wisdom come to mankind? How can we teach the spirit realm about His wisdom?

2. Imagine...the Church "will again be reverenced and admired." Is this possible? Explain your answer. What must the Church do to change its reputation? How must society change to accept the clear message the Church reveals?

3. What message does excellence in the Church speak to unbelievers? How will God's excellence create a new standard for all other excellence? Will we be criticized by those who don't understand God's perspective?

4. How does creativity within the Church bring a witness to the lost? How does this creativity manifest itself? How can the Church go beyond imitating the world's creativity and actually forge new paths?

5. In a dog-eat-dog environment, how will integrity make the Church stand above the rest? Won't Christians just get stepped on in the marketplace by those who play the political games to succeed? How will Christians' integrity make a way through the agendas of others?

6. Holiness is usually viewed as being a goody-two-shoes. How will society begin to see holiness for what it really is? Will they recognize the nature of God in us and desire it for themselves? What will bring about their desire?

MEDITATION

*"We will be a Church in which Jesus
is seen in His glory! It is the Holy Spirit's
presence and anointing that will dominate the
Christian's life. The Church will be radiant....
She will be a bride without spot or blemish"*
(*When Heaven Invades Earth*, Pages 182-183).

*What must you do to increase the Holy
Spirit's presence and the anointing in your
life? How will your local church need to prioritize
what it does to foster these throughout the congregation?*

Reaching the Maximum

❈

OF THE INCREASE OF HIS GOVERNMENT AND PEACE THERE WILL BE NO END, UPON THE THRONE OF DAVID AND OVER HIS KINGDOM, TO ORDER IT AND ESTABLISH IT WITH JUDGMENT AND JUSTICE FROM THAT TIME FORWARD, EVEN FOREVER. THE ZEAL OF THE LORD OF HOSTS WILL PERFORM THIS (ISAIAH 9:7).

❈

*A*ll Church history is built on partial revelation. Everything that has happened in the Church over the past 1900 years has fallen short of what the early Church had and lost. Each move of God has been followed by another, just to restore what was forfeited and forgotten. And we still haven't arrived to the standard that they attained, let alone surpassed it. Yet, not even the early Church fulfilled God's full intention for His people. That privilege was reserved for those in the last leg of the race. It is our destiny.

As wonderful as our spiritual roots are, they are insufficient. What was good for *yesterday* is deficient for *today*. To insist that we stay with what our fathers fought for is to insult our forefathers. They risked all to pursue something fresh and new in God. It's not that *everything* must change for us to flow with what God is saying and doing. It's just that we make too many assumptions about the *rightness* of what presently exists. Those assumptions blind us to the revelations still contained in Scripture. In reality, what we think of as the *normal Christian life* cannot hold the weight of what God is about to do. Our wineskins must change. There is very little of what we now know as Church life that will remain untouched in the next ten years.

(Quote From *When Heaven Invades Earth*, Pages 186-187)

QUESTIONS

1. Why does the Church have only partial revelation? Does God withhold His thoughts? Do we have problems hearing Him? What is the cause of our dilemma?

2. Why have we seen cycles of revival and forfeiture? Do you think there is a way to continue revival from one generation to the next? Do you think that is what our generation is supposed to do for the next?

3. What are your spiritual roots? Are there those in your family who have passed a heritage of the love of Christ to you? How have those roots affected your spiritual journey? What are their limitations?

4. Have you had an experience in revival or an increased anointing at any time in your life? If so, what made it so vibrant? Have you ever wanted to return to those feelings and experiences? Why doesn't God continue the same expressions and experiences throughout our journey? Why are we to pursue something fresh and new?

5. What do you think must change for us to flow with what God is saying and doing? What do you think it means when the author says, "We make too many assumptions about the rightness of what presently exists"? What are the assumptions the Church has made?

6. How does someone change a "wineskin"? What does this mean to you personally? How does the Church view their wineskin? What currently constitutes the "norm" for the Christian experience? Do you think God will dramatically make changes in that norm?

MEDITATION

"It has never entered the mind what God
has prepared for us while on this earth. His intent
is grand. Instead of limiting ourselves by our imagination
and experience, let's press on to a renewed hunger for things
yet to be seen. As we pursue the Extravagant One with
reckless abandon, we will discover that our greatest problem
is the resistance that comes from between our ears. But
faith is superior. And it's time for us to make Him
unconcerned about whether or not He'll find faith on the earth"
(*When Heaven Invades Earth*, Page 187).

Flip through the pages of this book and highlight
any comments, questions, or answers that you need
to follow up on, in the coming days. Take a protracted
time to pray over your part in seeing Heaven invade Earth!

NOTES

NOTES

NOTES

NOTES

NOTES

NOTES

NOTES

NOTES

NOTES

NOTES

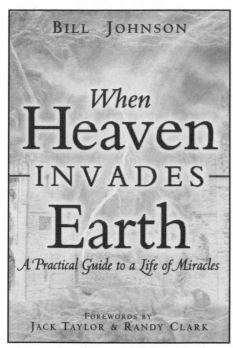

WHEN HEAVEN INVADES EARTH

Bill Johnson

When Heaven Invades Earth is a powerful statement and testimony on the Kingdom of God. Theologically sound, well supported, and extremely well argued, this message provides a carefully constructed biblical foundation for the average Christian to live and walk in the miraculous, supernatural power of God. Not only is the supernatural possible, it is also our commission. The Great Commission that Christ gave to the Church challenges us and makes us responsible to rise up to this supreme supernatural calling. Johnson shows you how you are called to dominion in the earth through the divine rule of God.

0-7684-2952-8 $13.99